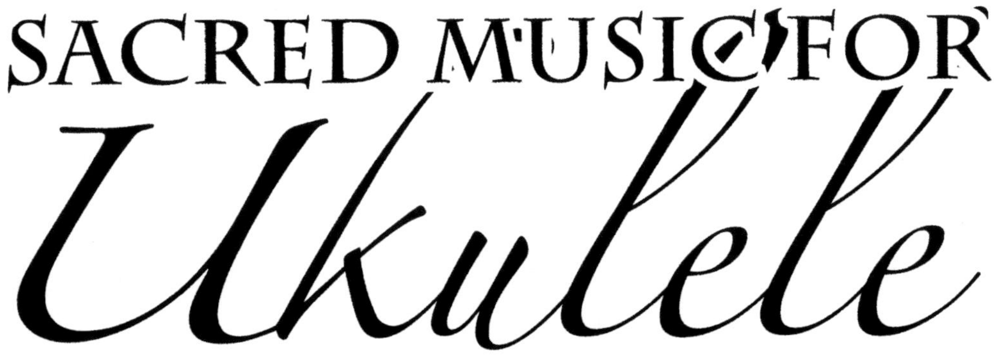

TABLATURE METHOD BOOK

BY MARY LOU STOUT DEMPLER

Cover Photo courtesy of The Music Link Corporation/Johnson Guitars
www.johnsongtr.com

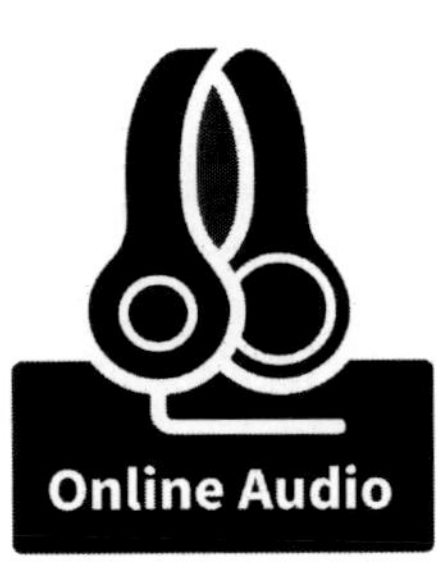

www.melbay.com/21094BCDEB

Audio Contents

1. Amazing Grace
2. He's Got The Whole World In His Hands
3. Holy, Holy, Holy
4. Do, Lord
5. Rock of Ages
6. All Night, All Day
7. Kum Ba Ya
8. Down by the Riverside
9. Simple Gifts
10. Abide with Me
11. When The Saints Go Marching In
12. Angel of God

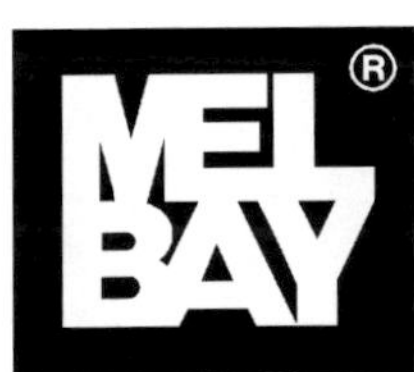

Visit us on the Web at www.melbay.com — E-mail us at email@melbay.com

Sacred Music for Ukulele

CONTENTS

Psalm 9:2
I will praise you Lord, with all my heart; I will declare all your wondrous deeds.

Dear Reader,

God has given each of us the gift of music. Whether we listen to music or play music, it is still God's gift to us. He has blessed me abundantly. I want to, "Praise the Lord," " give thanks, dedicate every note to His honor and glory" and share my blessings with you. In this Easy Ukulele Gospel Tablature Method Book you can play the melody instantly without reading music, just by following the tablature. The ukulele has a wonderful harp-like sound and is perfect for Gospel music. As you play the melody or chords, be sure to sing along and "Praise the Lord"

Musically Yours,

Mary Lou Stout Dempler

The Louisville Ukulele Association Unlimited (LUAU) has gathered together to play the songs in this book and recorded the "Praise the Lord" audio. The audio recording is available so you can play along with LUAU.

Acknowledgements

I declare all God's wondrous deeds; for creating me in His image and likeness: Jesus for saving me; the Holy Spirit for leading me on paths I should go; to the one God created for me, my husband and very best friend Shane.

The Ukulele

Tuning Pegs
Head Stock
Nut
Frets
Neck
Fret Marks
Sound Hole
Body
Bridge

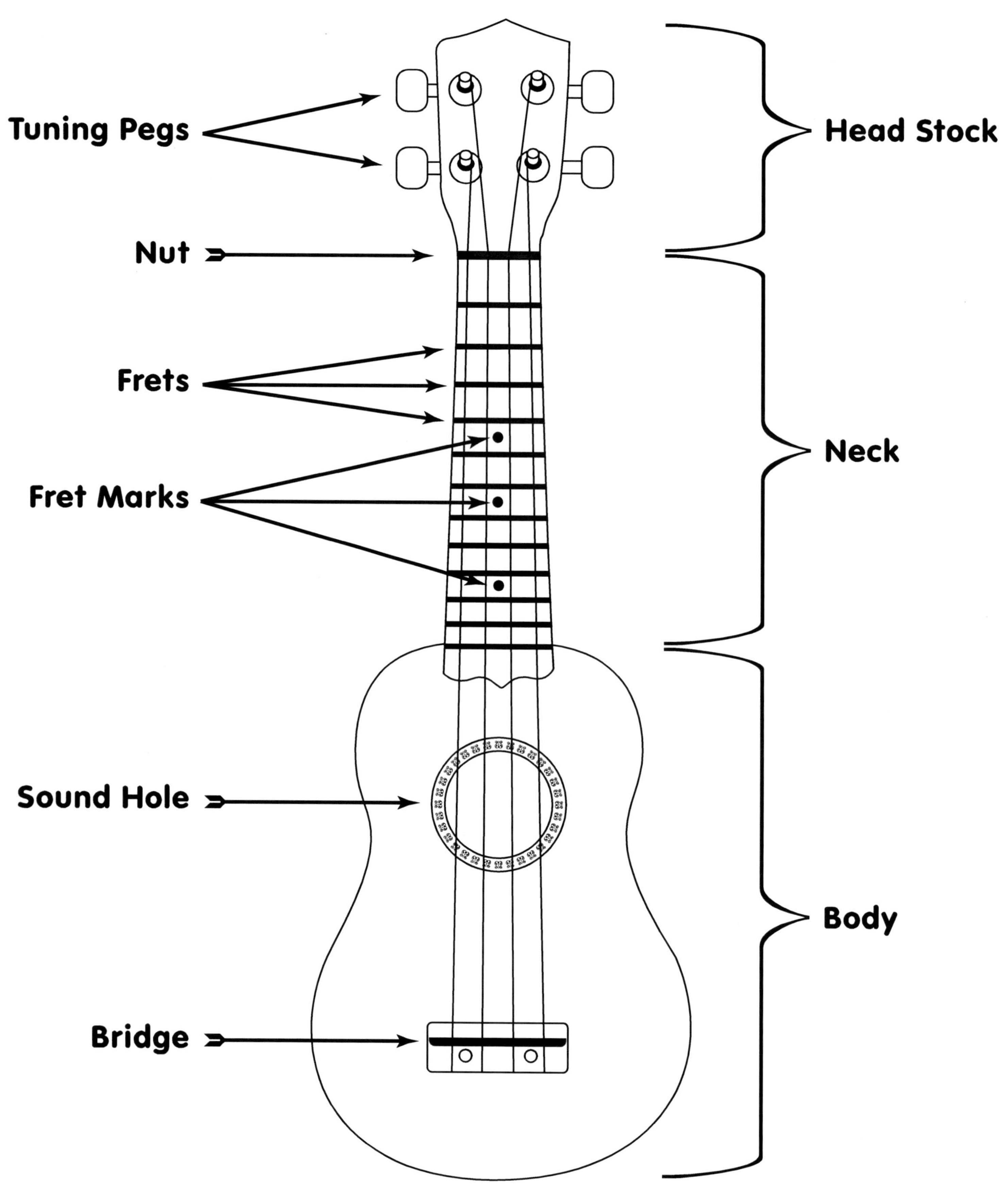

How to Tune the Ukulele

The easiest way to tune the Ukulele is with a Uke pitch pipe. **G C E A** tuning is the most widely used tuning and is the easiest to play. This method only uses **G C E A** tuing because it is easier to play in the keys of **F B♭ E♭** and **A♭**. **A D F♯ B** tuning is different although the chords are the same, the chord names have been changed. Purchase a **G C E A** pitch pipe and tune to the diagram.

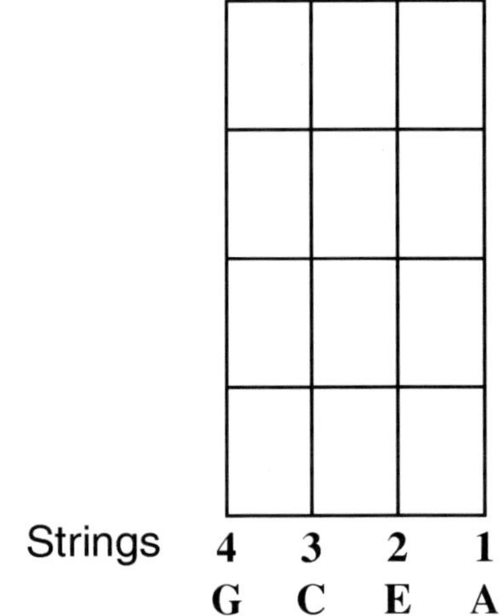

Tuning the Uke using a piano

begin with middle **C** for the third string

E for the second string

G for the fourth string

A for the first string.

Tuning the Uke without a pitch pipe or piano

If a pitch pipe or piano is not available, it can be tuned by ear. First, approximate an **A** on the first string.

Press the **fifth fret** of the second string to equal the pitch of the **first string A.**

Press the **fourth fret** of the third string to equal the pitch of the **second string E.**

Press the **second fret** of the fourth string to equal the pitch of the **first string A.**

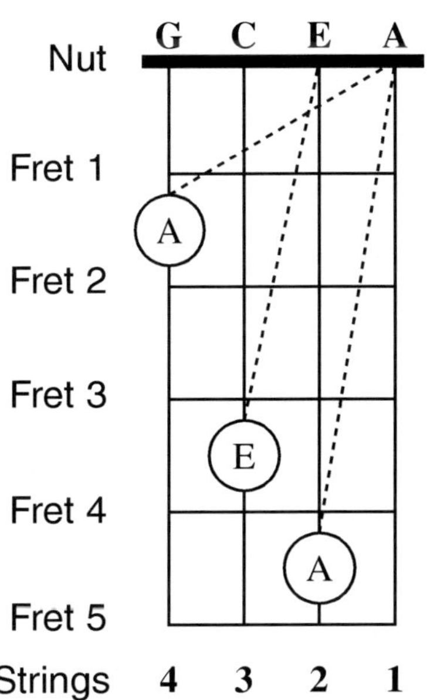

How to Hold the Uke

When playing the Uke hold the Head Stock at the 2 o'clock position and the bottom of the body at the 7 o'clock position. Press the body of the Uke firmly against your chest. Press fingers firmly on the fret board. Do not touch the strings when forming left hand finger positions for notes or chords.

Hand and Finger Positions for the Uke

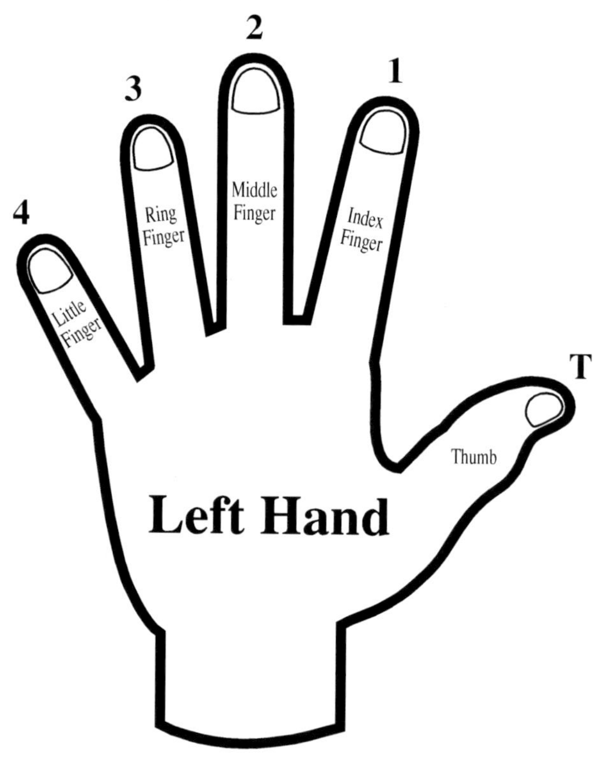

The left hand holds the neck of the uke. The thumb is behind the neck, wrist relaxed, and hand is arched over the strings.

The **first finger** (index) plays notes on the **first fret.**

The **second finger** (middle) plays notes on the **second fret.**

The **third finger** (ring) plays notes on the **third fret.**

The **fourth finger** (little) plays notes on the **fourth fret.**

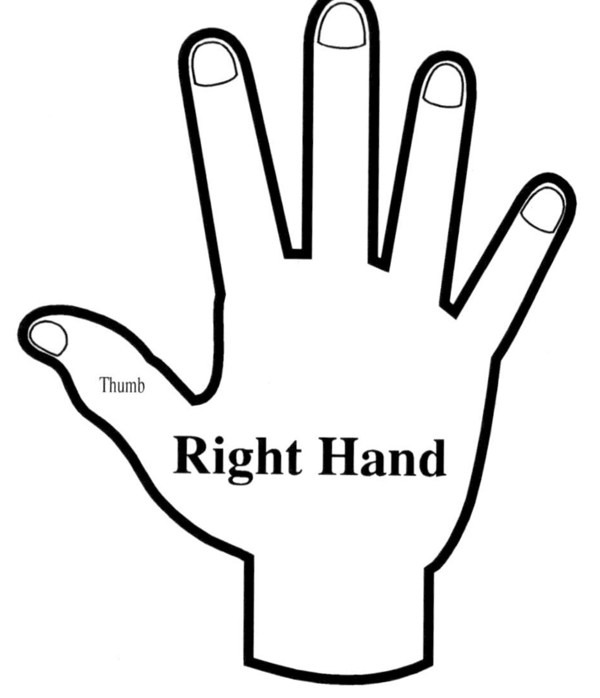

The right hand strums the strings. Use a pick or the thumb to strum. A down stroke is indicated with the symbol ⊓ (down stroke). An up stroke is indicated with the symbol V (up stroke).

How to Read Tablature

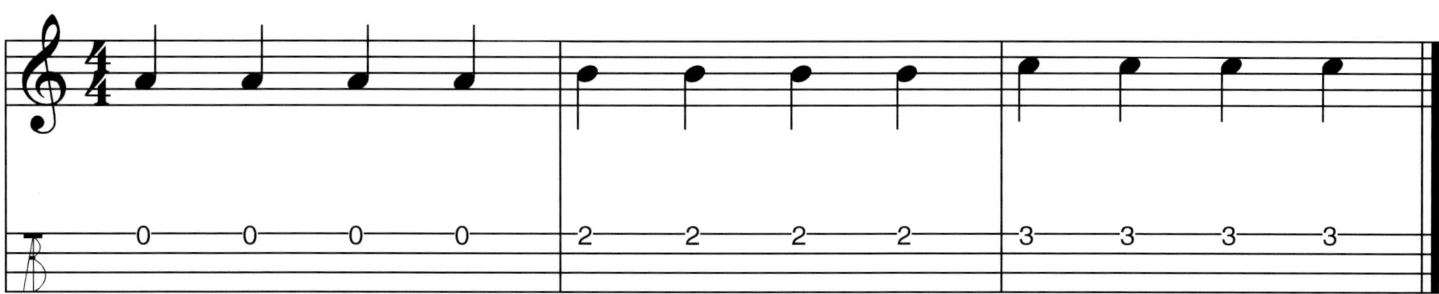

Tablature is a simple diagram of the ukulele fretboard. The lines in Tablature represent each string. The number on the string indicates the fret that is played on that string to sound the note written on the staff. In the example above, the first measure of the staff contains four A notes. The Tablature example below the staff indicates the position of the A notes. Play the first string 0 (0 = open, do not finger any fret) four times. The bar lines that separate the measures of the tablature correspond with the bar lines on the music staff. The second measure contains four B notes found on the first string, at the second fret, played four times. The third measure is four C notes, found on the first string, at the third fret, played four times. Tablature is not a substitute for the staff. It is a diagram (map) to locate notes on the ukulele fretboard.

The top line of the tablature is string 1, the A string.

The second line is string 2, the E string.

The third line is string 3, the C string.

The bottom line of the tablature is string 4, the G string.

Chord Diagrams

In order to play a chord, place your fingers as indicated on the chord diagram. The strings are the vertical lines and the frets are the horizontal lines. The circles with numbers indicated the position of the left hand fingers. Place fingers firmly on the fret to produce a clear sound. Do not place fingers directly on top of the fret bar. Open strings require no fingers on the fret board. Open strings are represented by the circles below the string numbers.

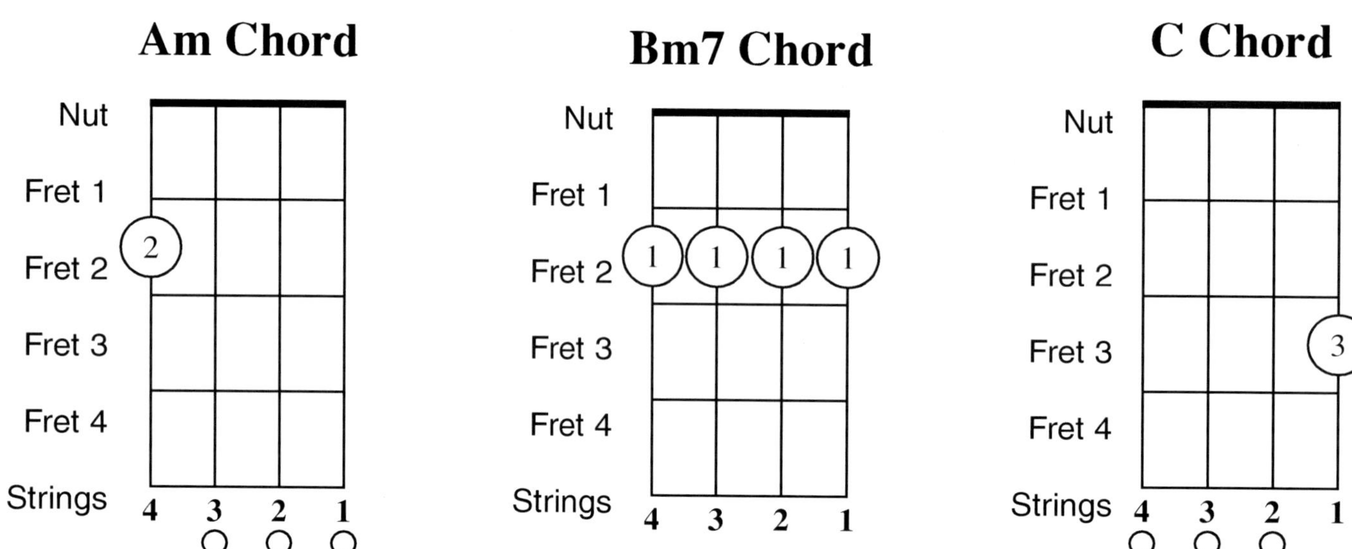

D Chord

Nut
Fret 1
Fret 2
Fret 3
Fret 4
Strings 4 3 2 1
1 2 3

D7 Chord

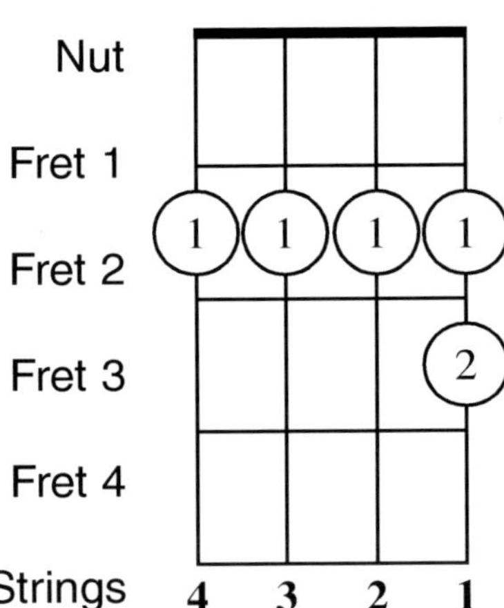

Dm Chord

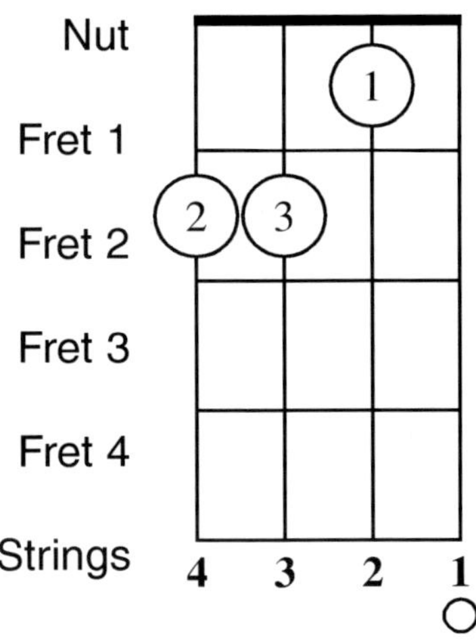

Em Chord

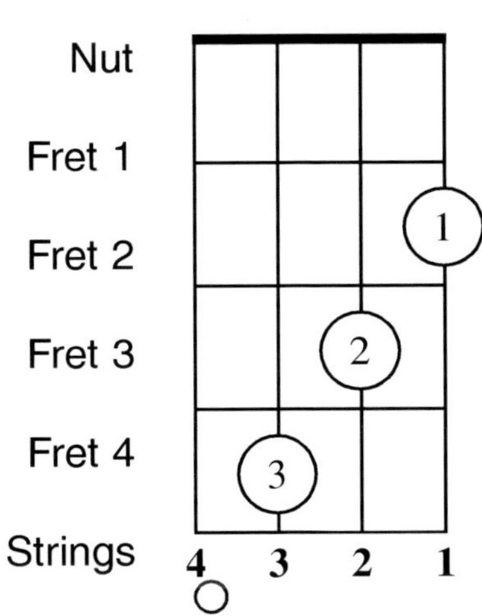

F Chord

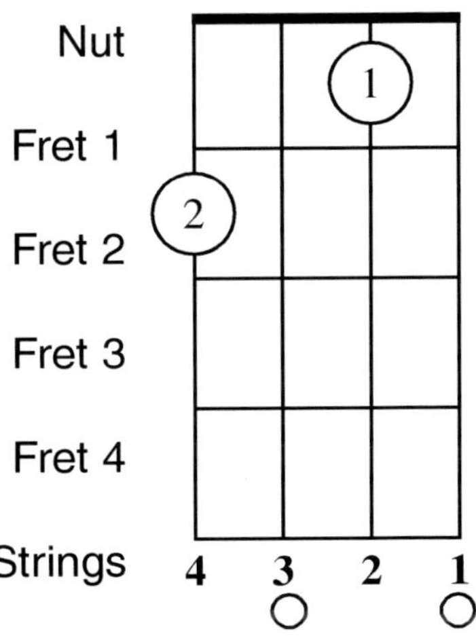

G Chord

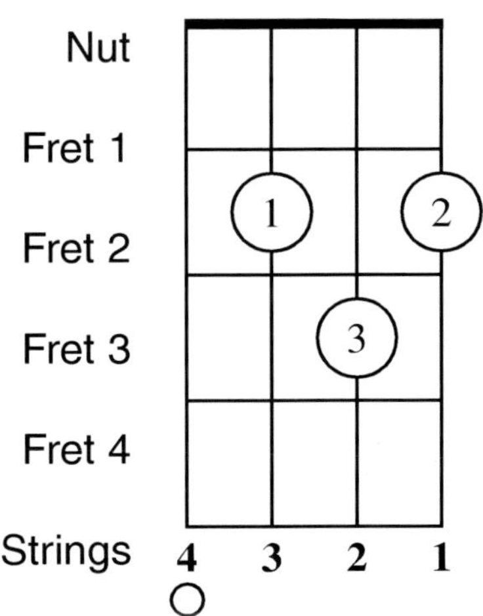

G7 Chord

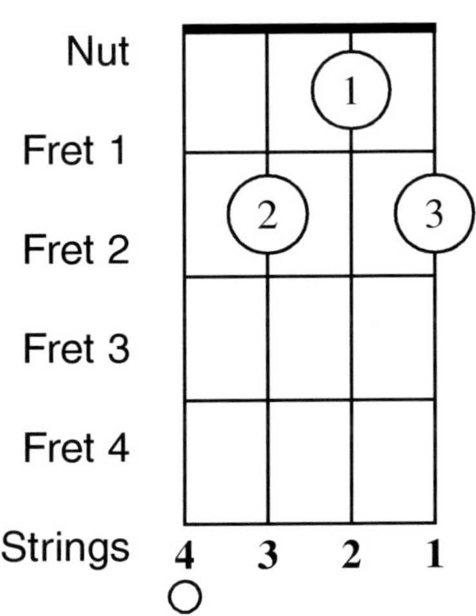

Amazing Grace

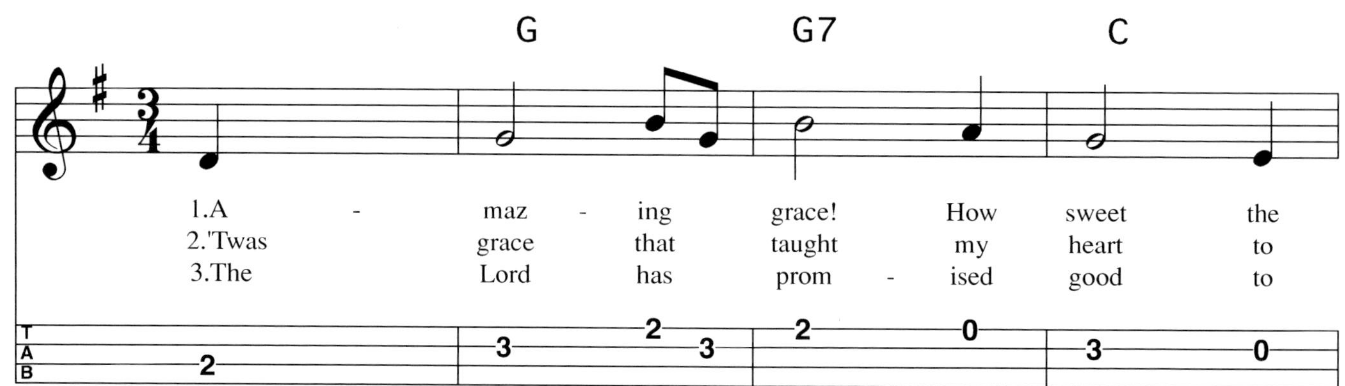

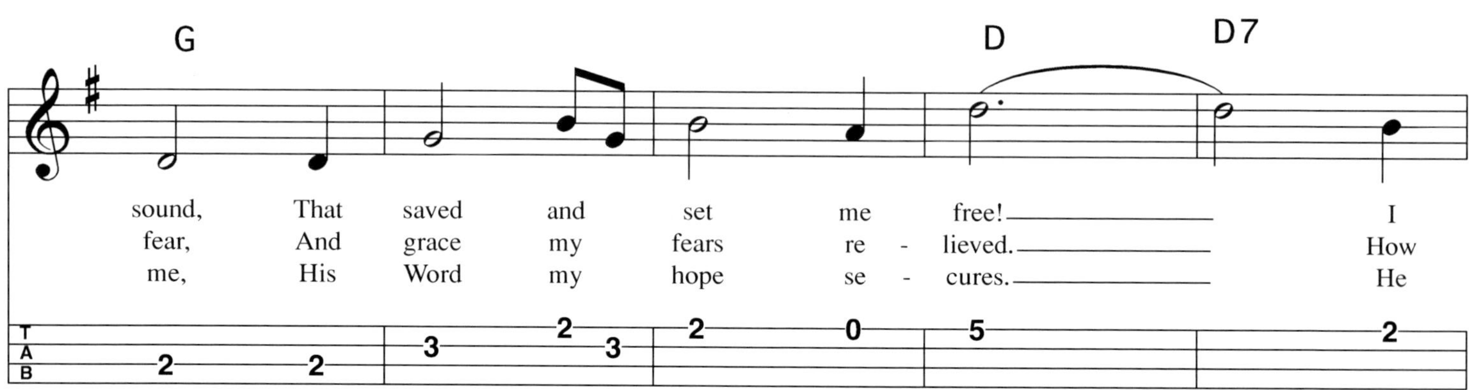

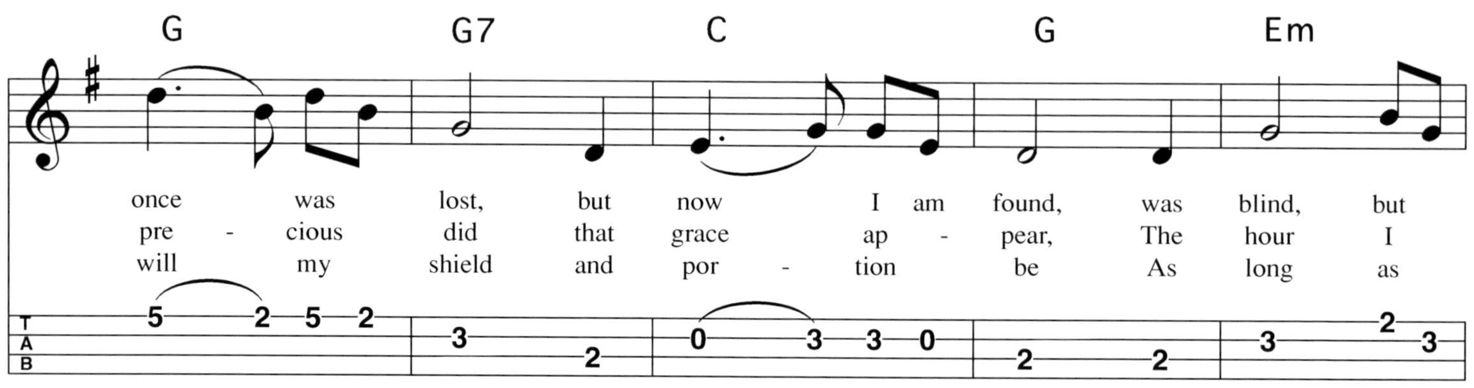

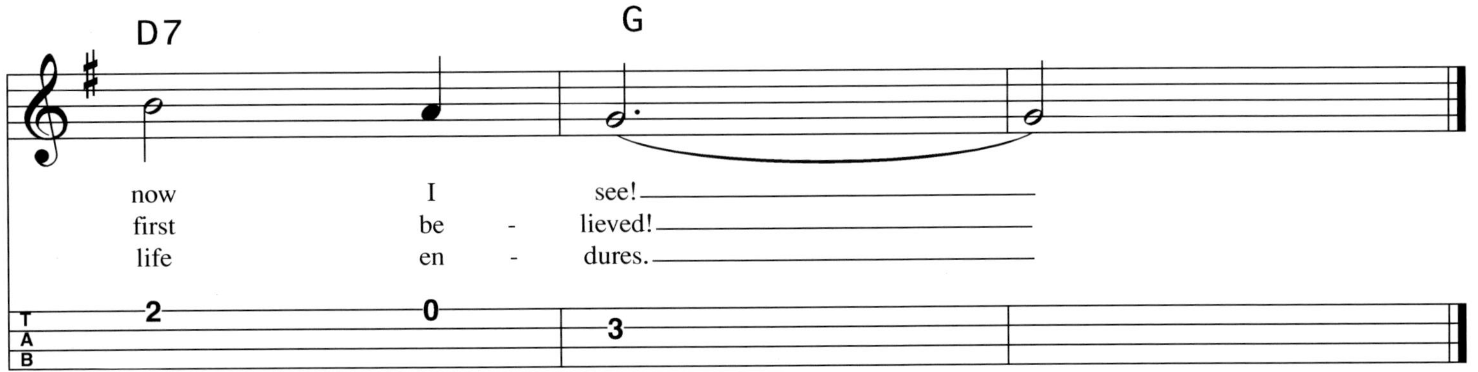

4.Thru many dangers, toils and snares, I have already come.
His grace has brought me safe thus far, His grace will lead me home.

5.Yes, when this flesh and heart shall fail and mortal life shall cease,
Amazing grace shall then prevail in heaven's joy and peace.

6.When we've been there ten thousand years, bright shining as the sun,
we've no less days to sing God's praise than when we'd first begun.

He's Got the Whole World in His Hands

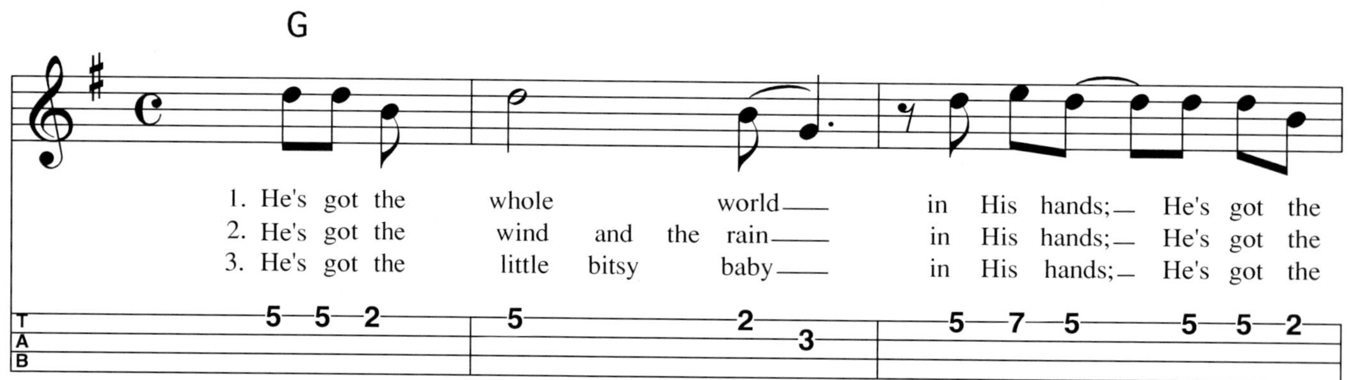

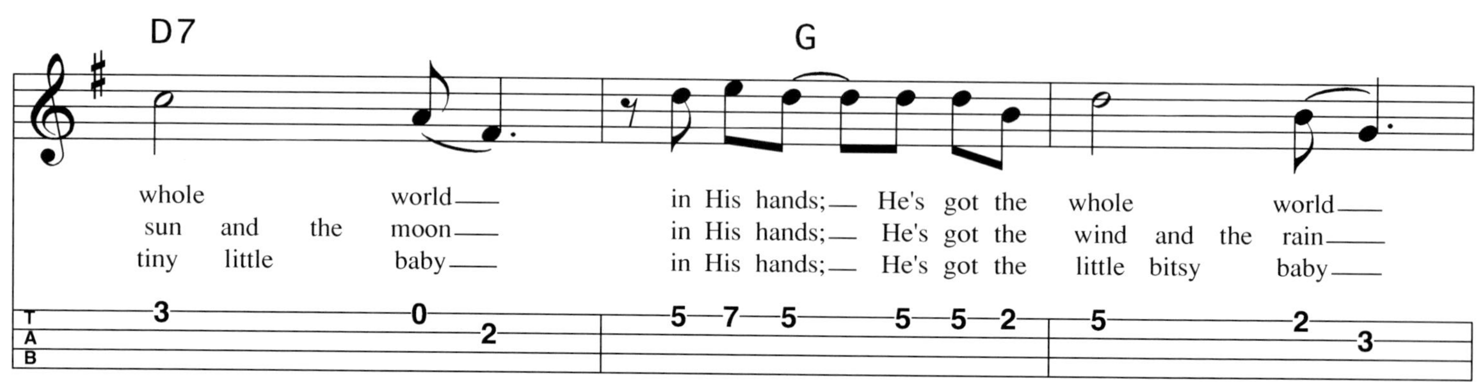

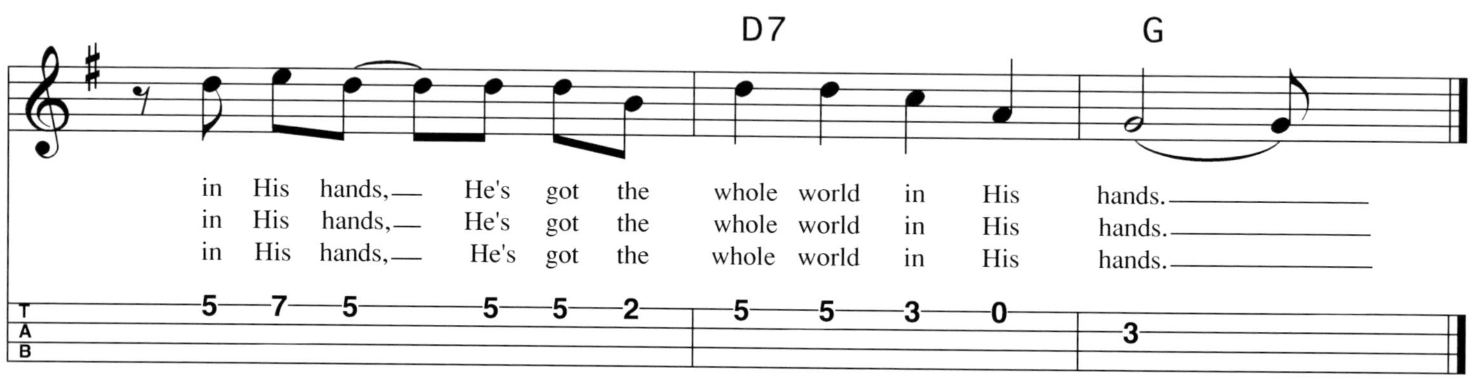

4.He's got the Military families in His hands;
He's got the Military families in His hands;
He's got the Military families in His hands,
He's got the whole world in His hands.

5.Repeat First Verse

Holy, Holy, Holy

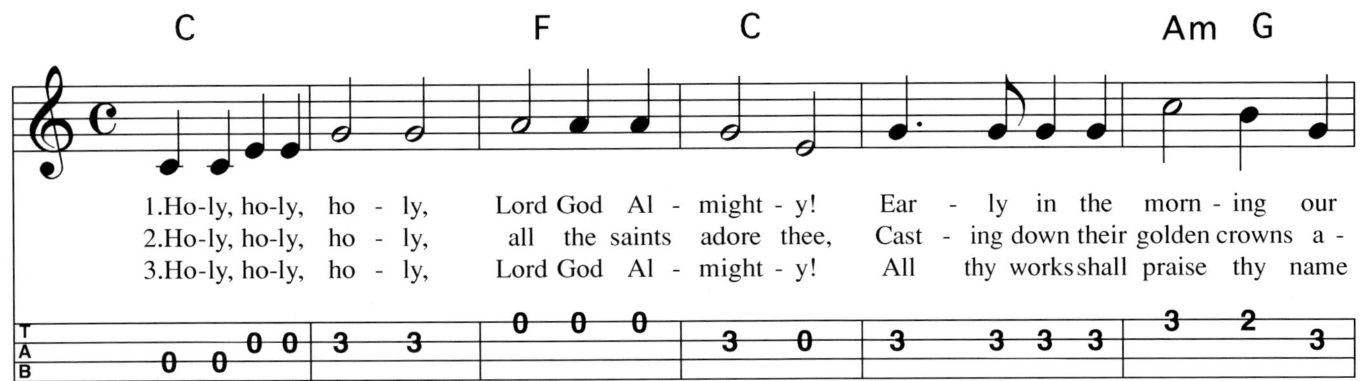

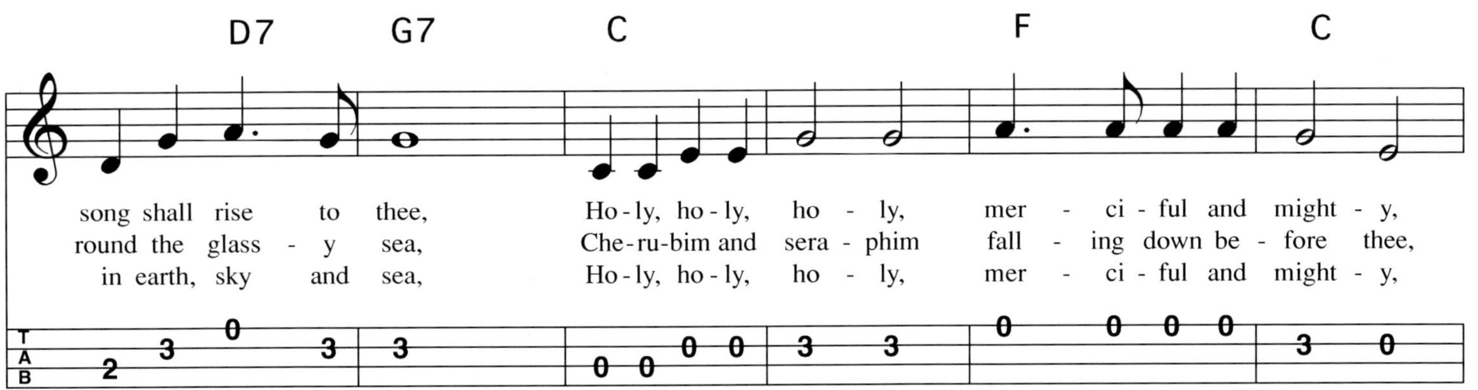

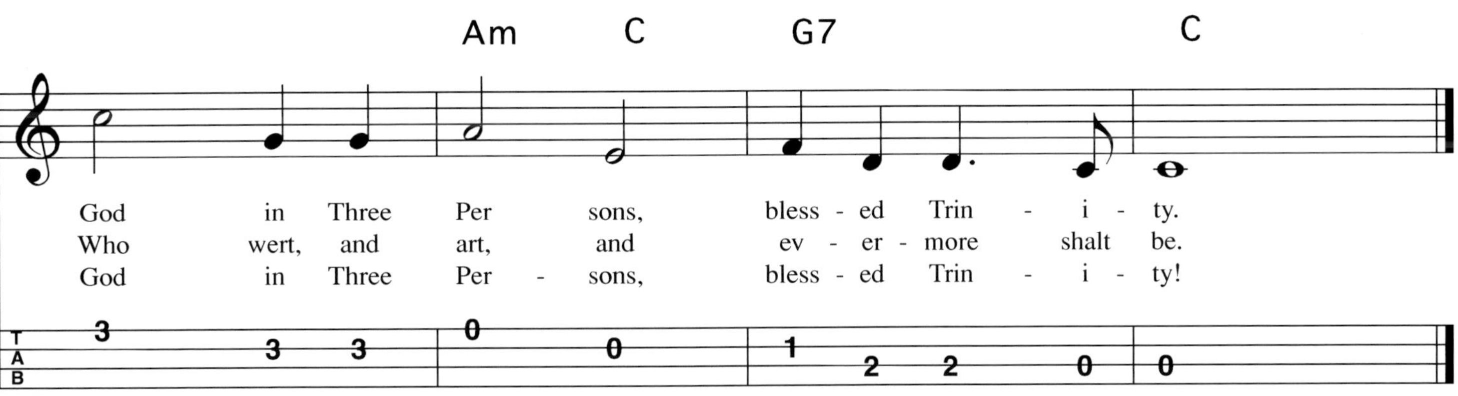

Do, Lord

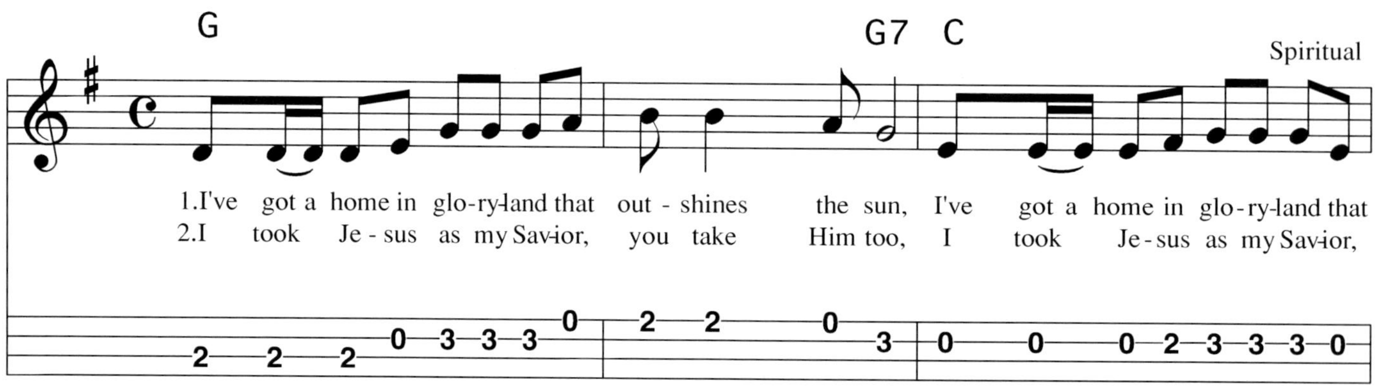
G
G7
C
Spiritual
1.I've got a home in glo-ry-land that out - shines the sun, I've got a home in glo-ry-land that
2.I took Je - sus as my Sav-ior, you take Him too, I took Je-sus as my Sav-ior,

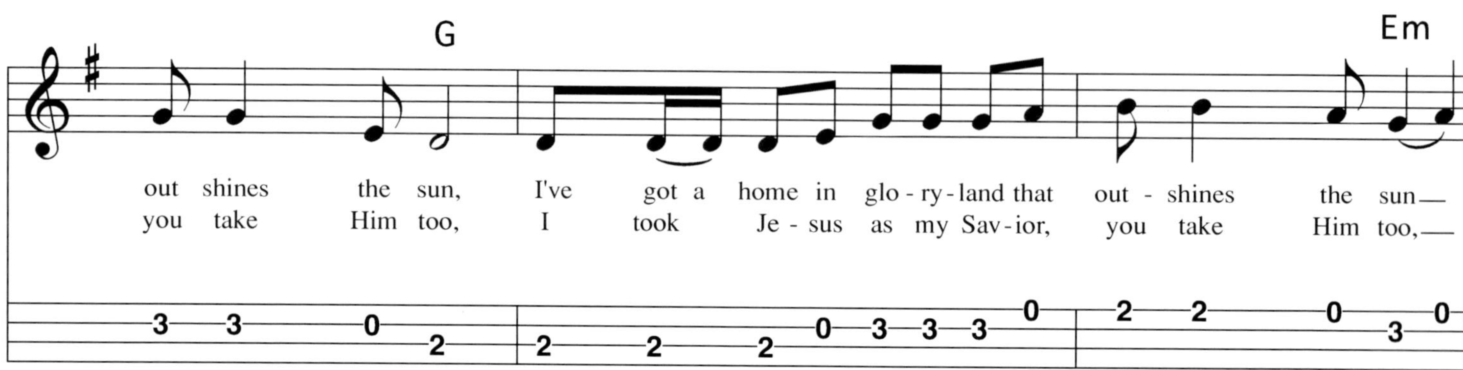
G
Em
out shines the sun, I've got a home in glo - ry - land that out - shines the sun
you take Him too, I took Je - sus as my Sav - ior, you take Him too,

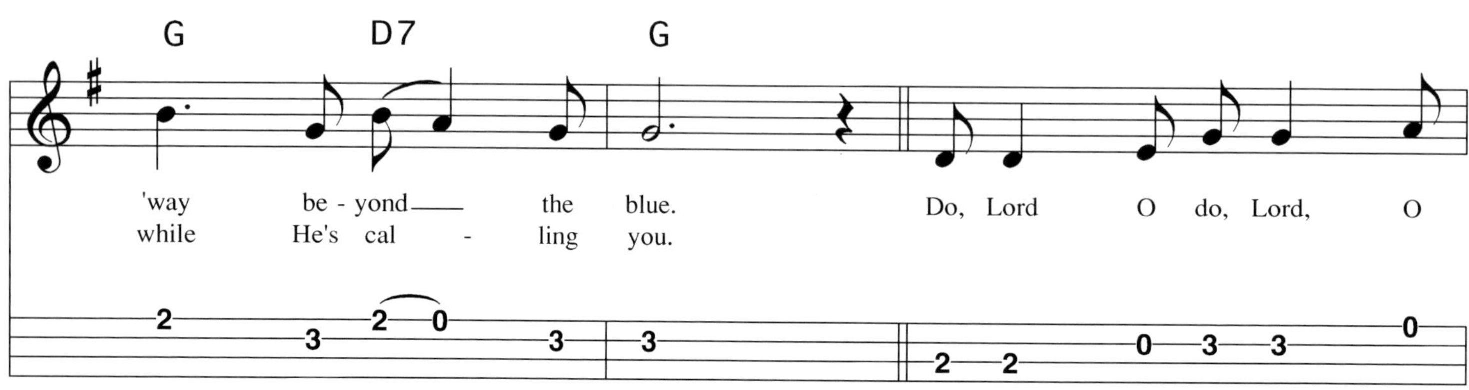
G
D7
G
'way be - yond the blue. Do, Lord O do, Lord, O
while He's cal - ling you.

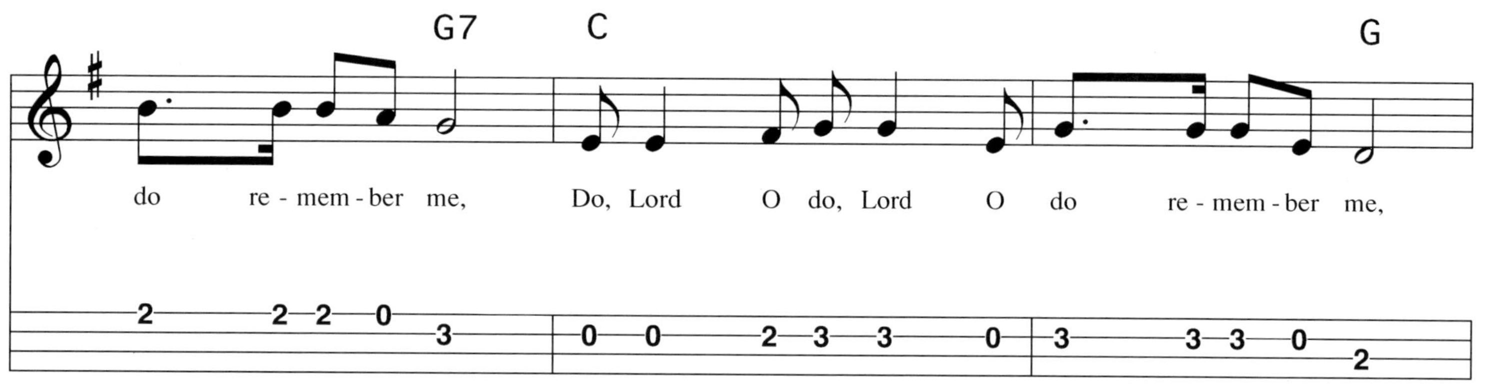
G7
C
G
do re - mem - ber me, Do, Lord O do, Lord O do re - mem - ber me,
2 2 2 0 3 0 0 2 3 3 0 3 3 3 0 2

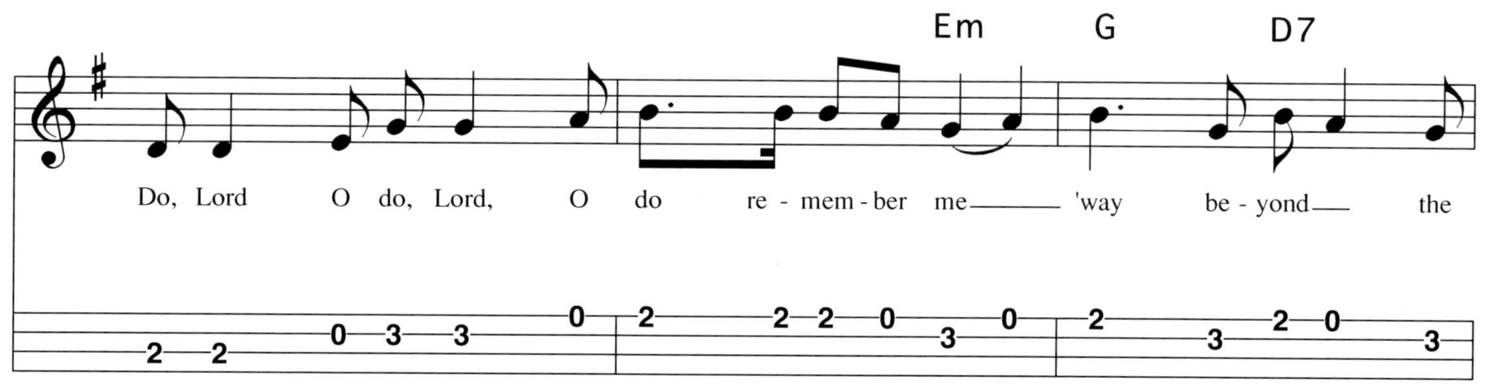
Em
G
D7
Do, Lord O do, Lord, O do re - mem - ber me 'way be - yond the
2 2 0 3 3 0 2 2 2 0 3 0 2 3 2 0 3

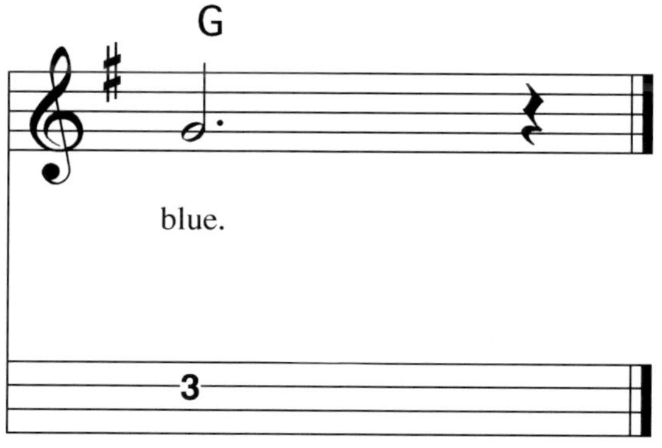
G
blue.
3

Rock of Ages

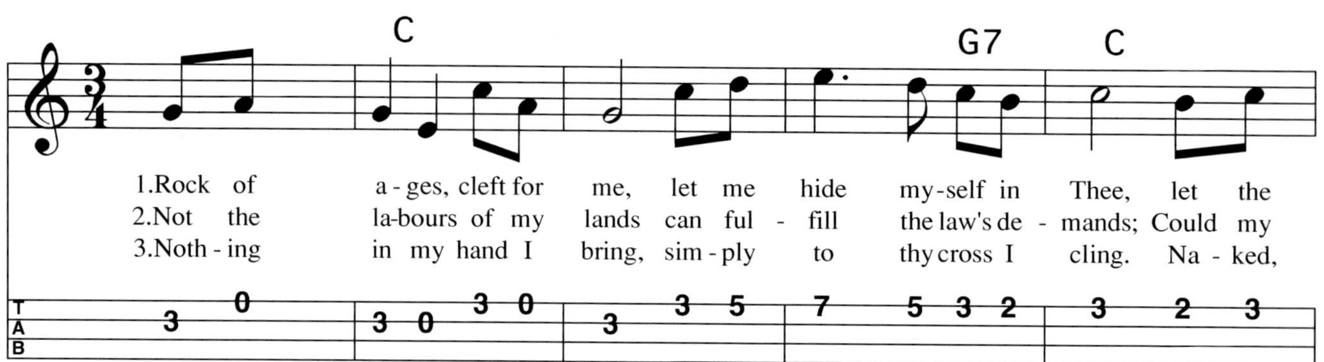

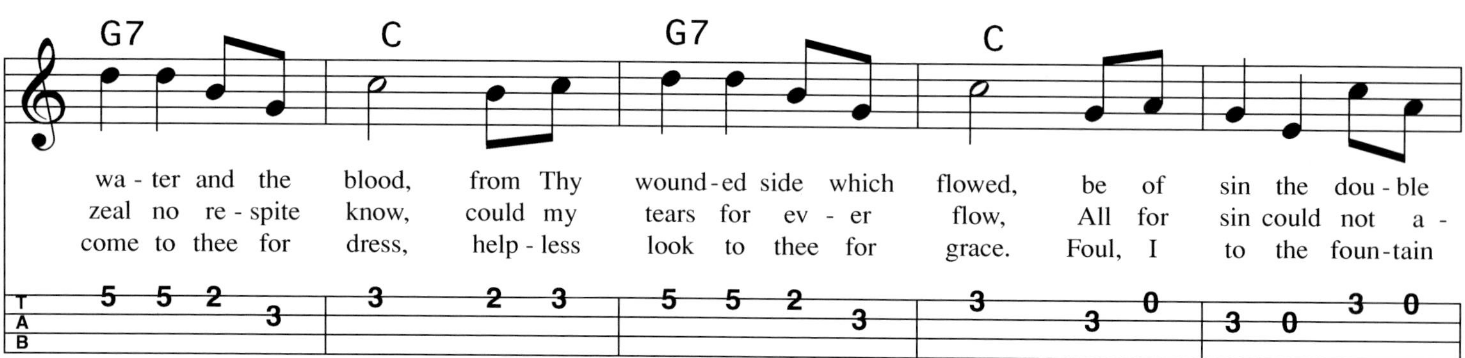

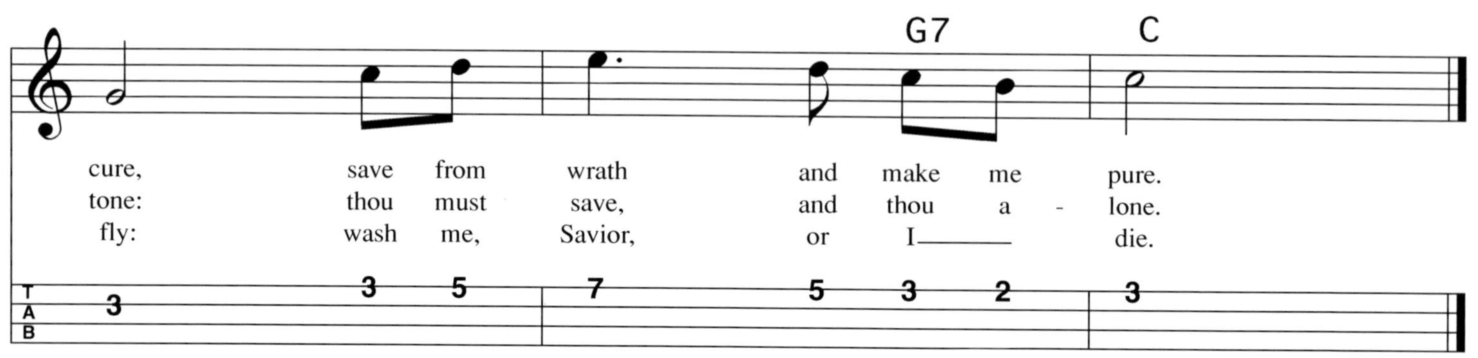

4.While I draw this fleeting breath,
when my eyelids close in death.
While I soar to worlds unknown,
see thee on thy judgment throne,
Rock of Ages, cleft for me,
let me hide myself in thee.

All Night, All Day

Spiritual

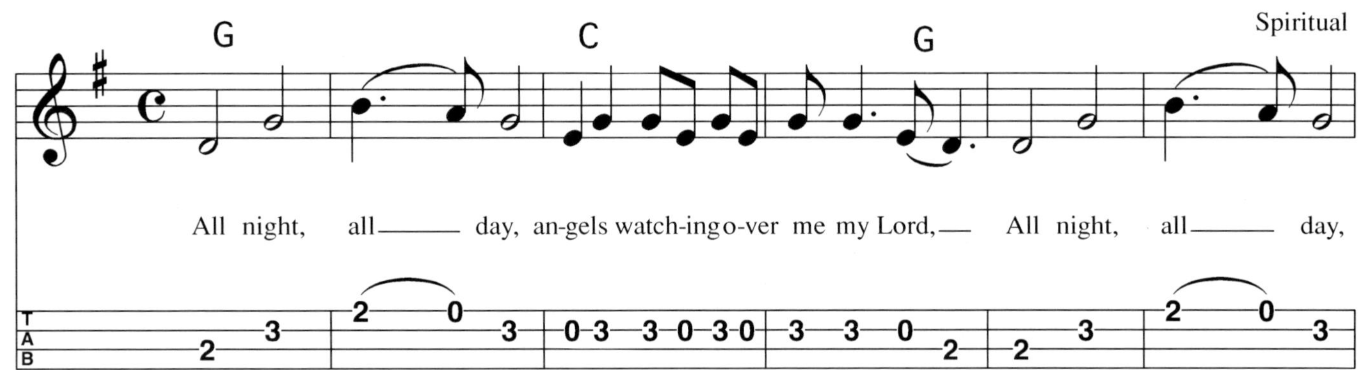

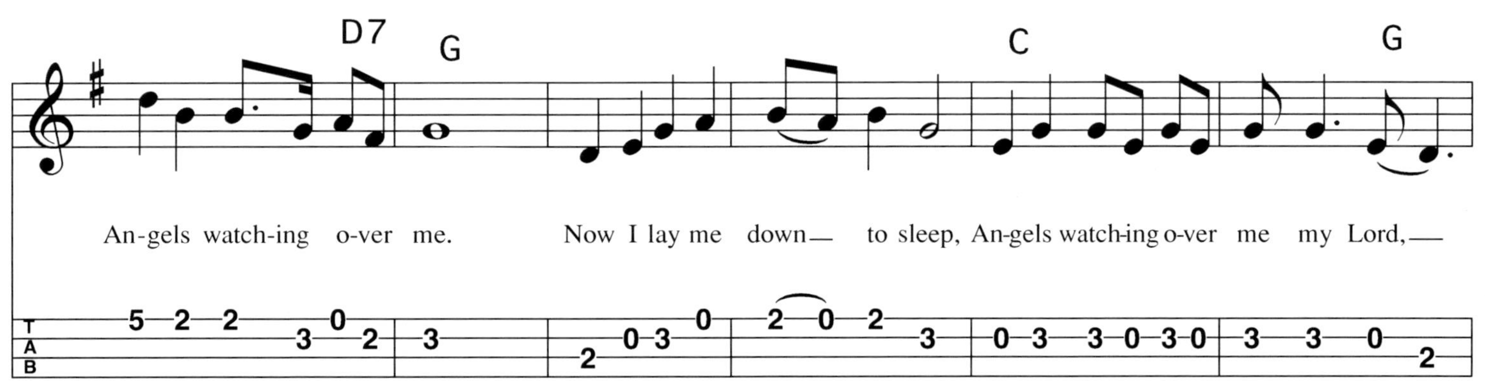

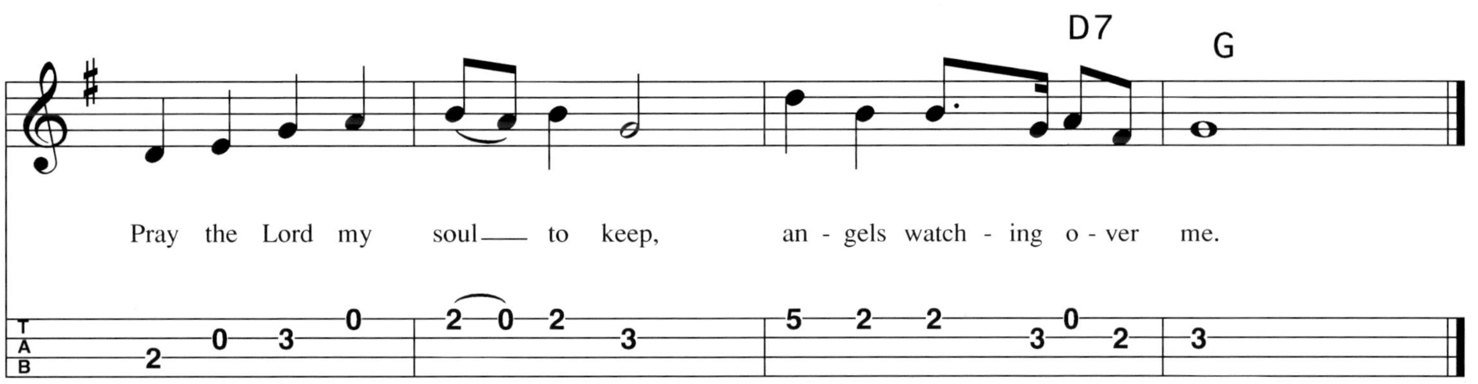

Kum Ba Yah

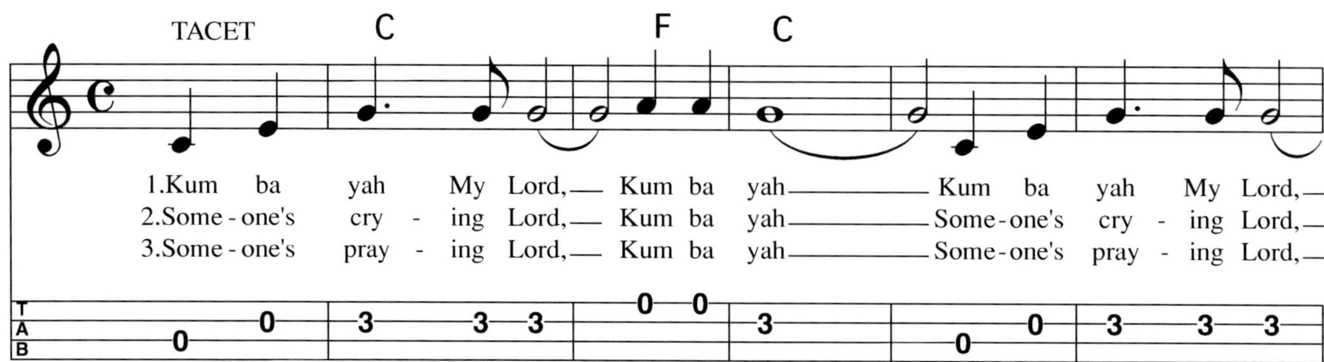

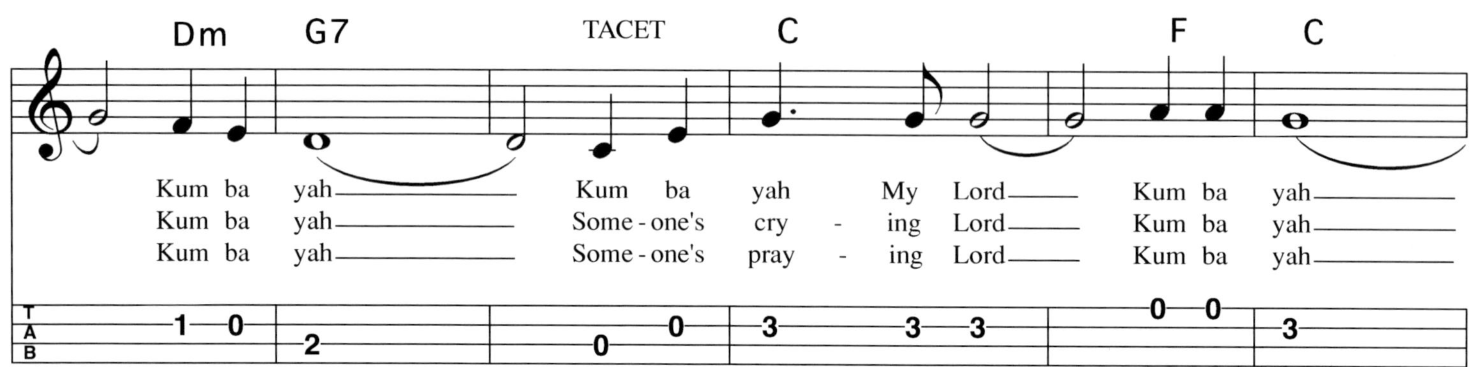

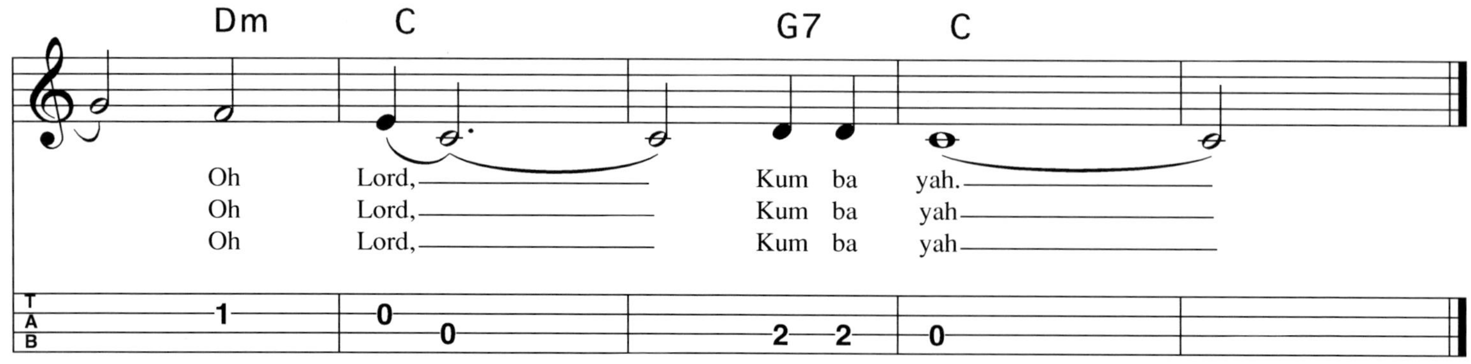

4.Someone's singing Lord, Kum ba yah
Someone's singing Lord, Kum ba yah
Someone's singing Lord, Kum ba yah
Oh Lord, Kum ba yah

Down by the Riverside

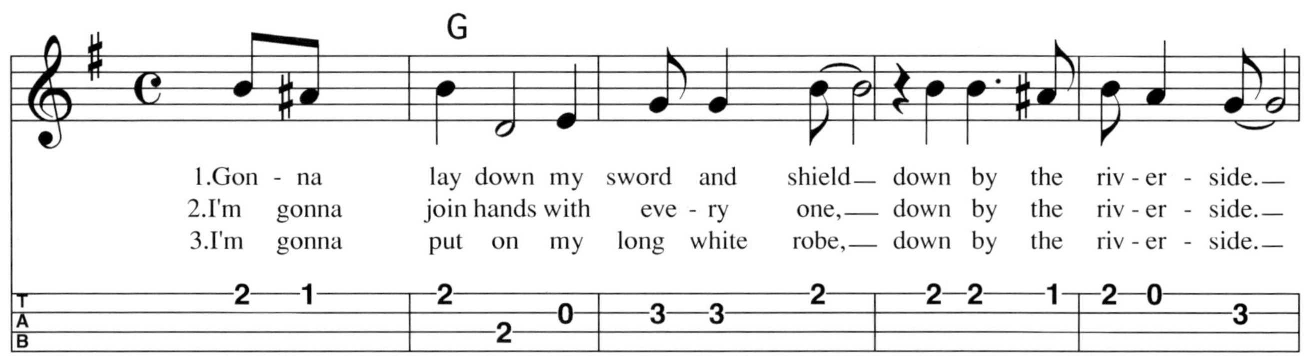

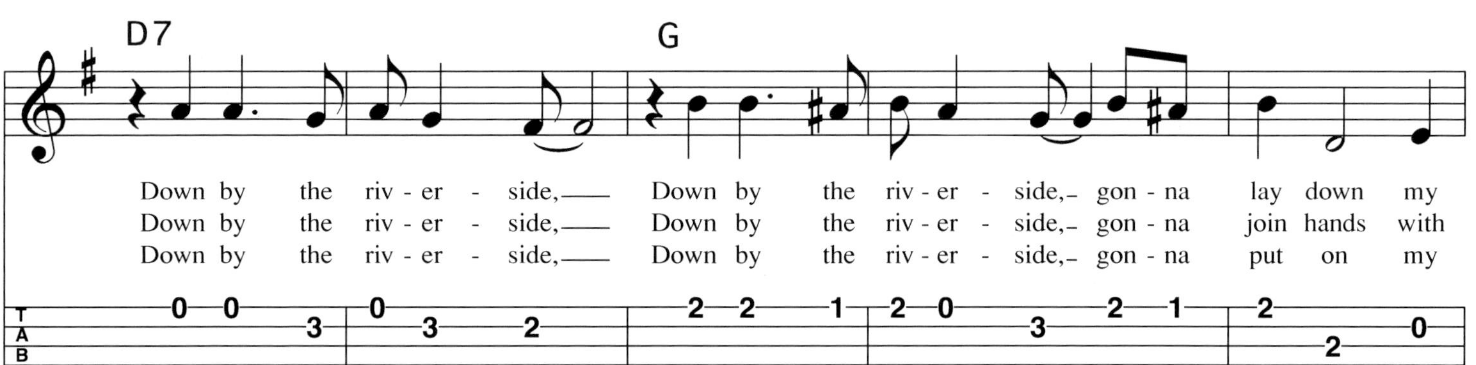

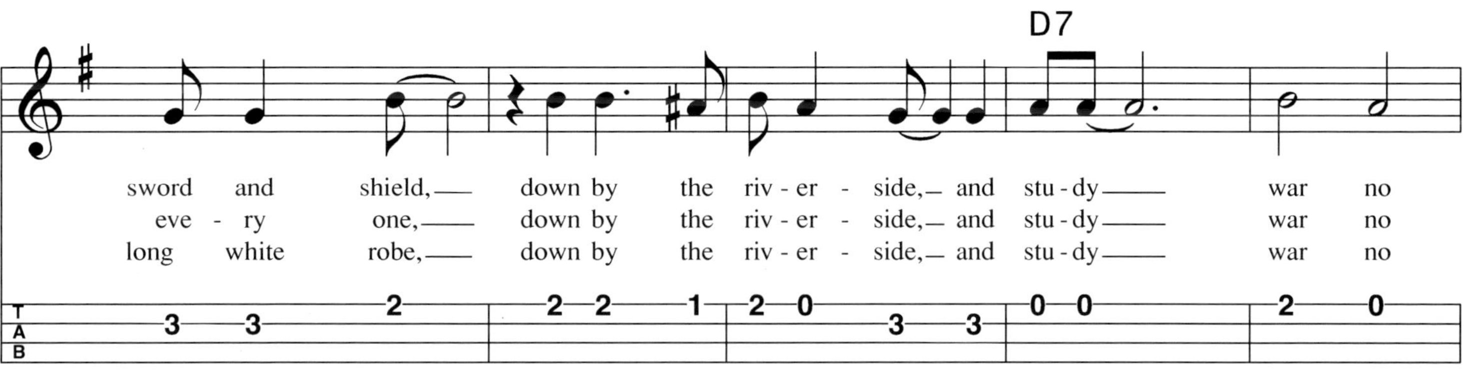

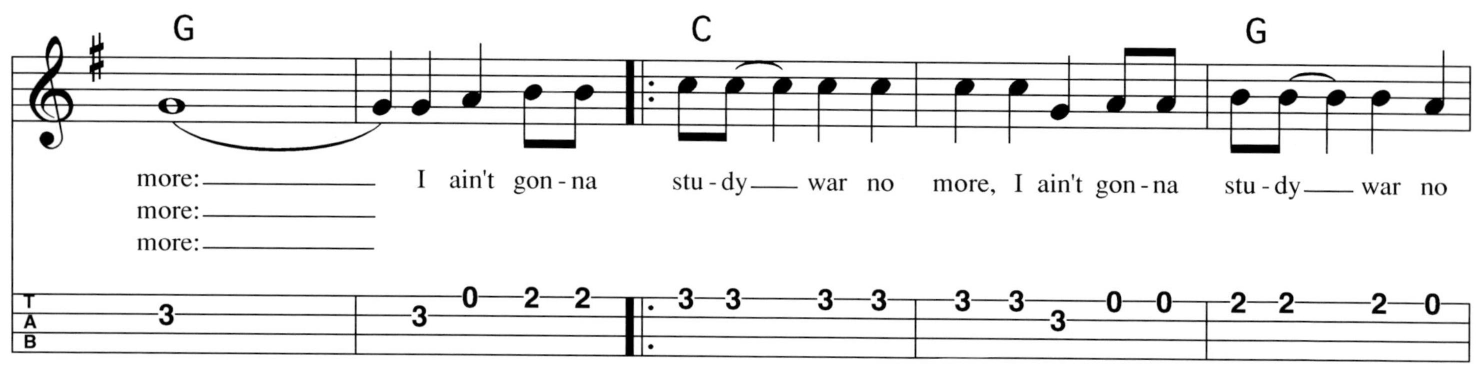
G
C
G
more:
more:
more:
I ain't gon - na
stu - dy war no
more, I ain't gon - na
stu - dy war no
T
A
B
3
3 0 2 2
3 3 3 3
3 3 3 0 0
2 2 2 0

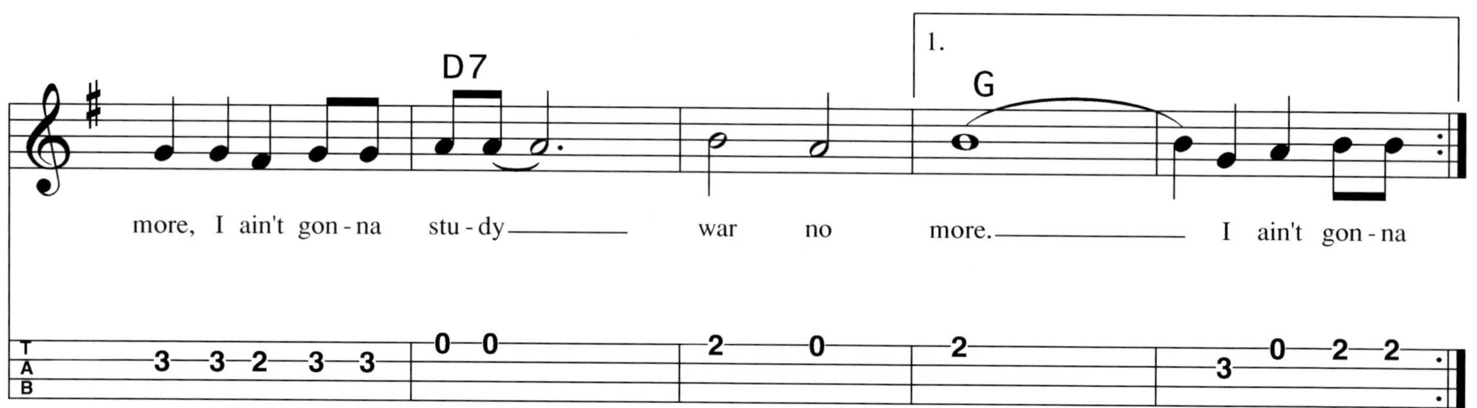
D7
1.
G
more, I ain't gon - na
stu - dy
war no
more.
I ain't gon - na
T
A
B
3 3 2 3 3
0 0
2 0
2
3 0 2 2

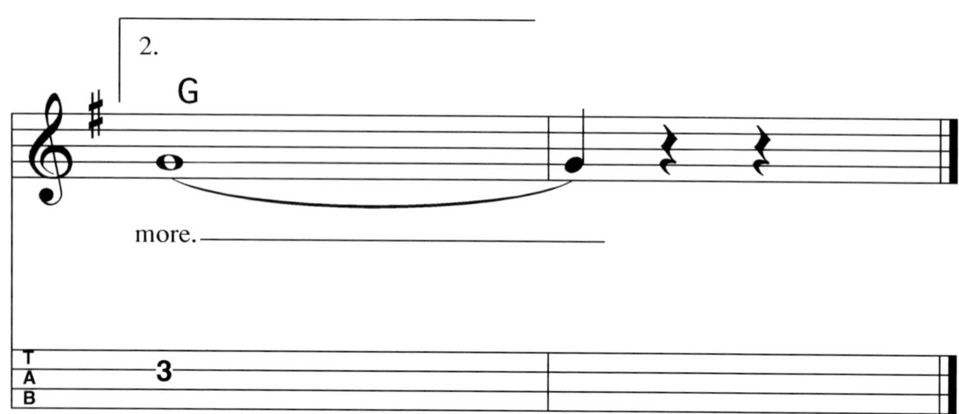
2.
G
more.
T
A
B
3

Simple Gifts

Shaker Song

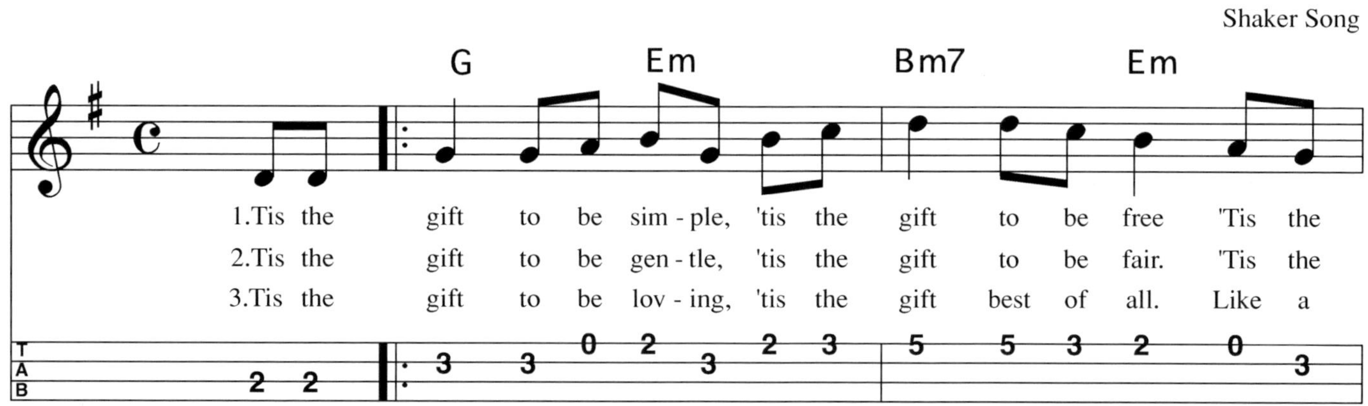

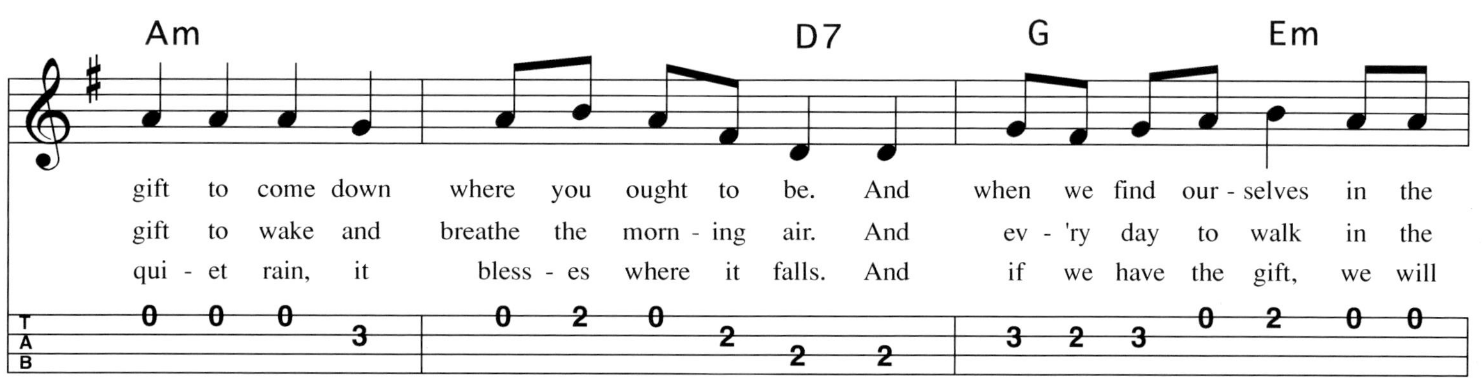

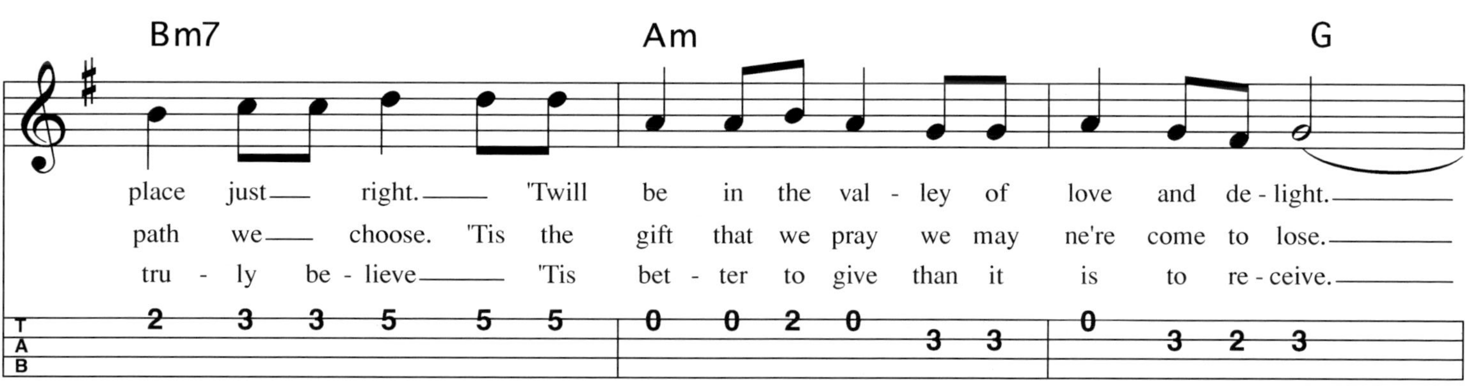

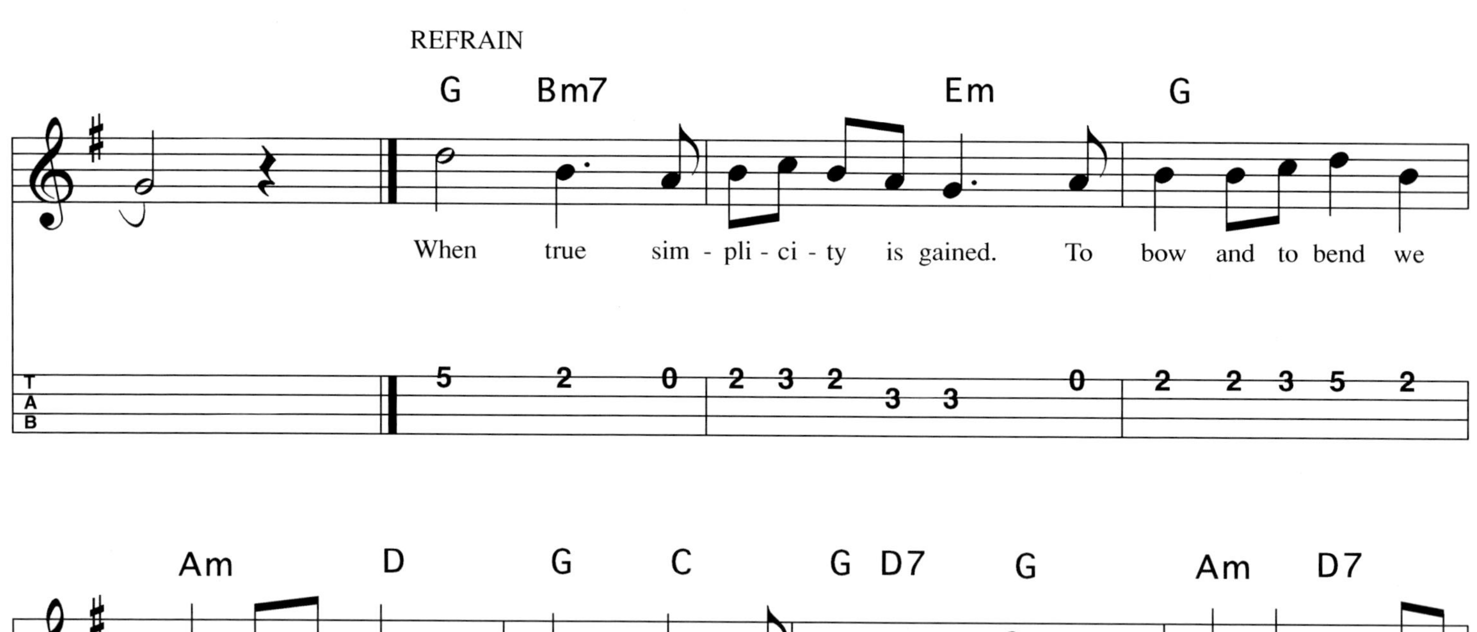

Am D G C G D7 G Am D7
shan't be a - shamed. To turn, turn will be our de - light, 'Til by turn - ing, turn - ing we
T
A
B
0 0 2 0 2 3 3 0 2 2 3 5 3 2 0 0 2 2 0

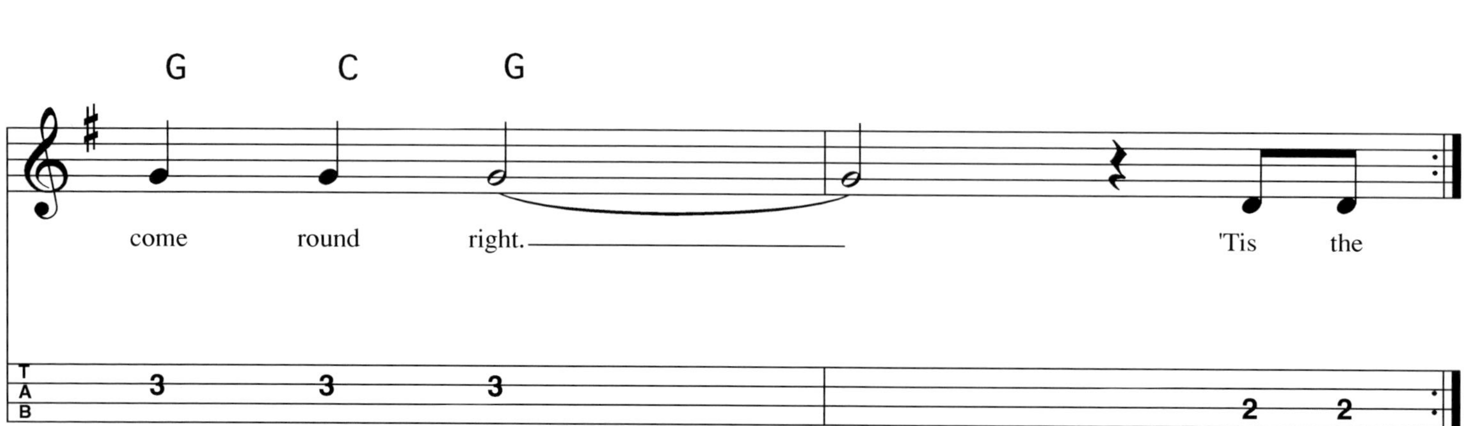

Abide with Me

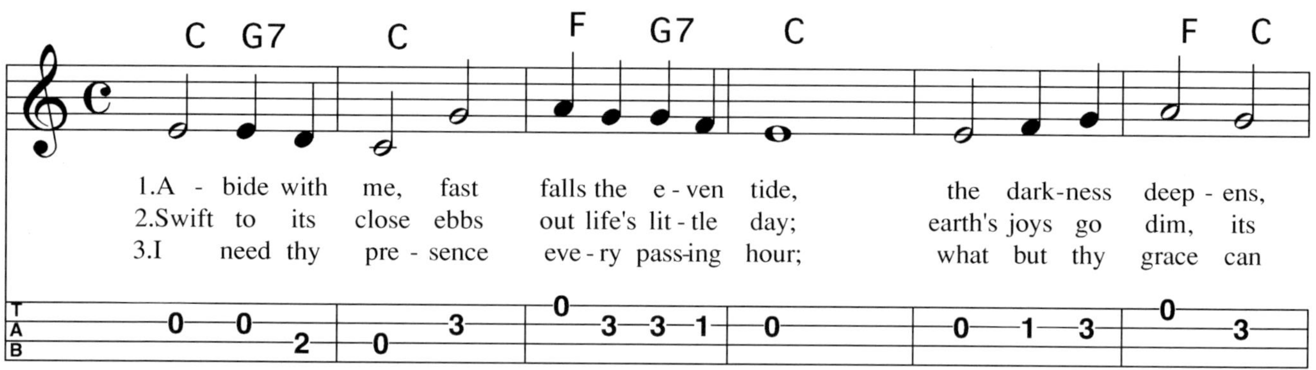

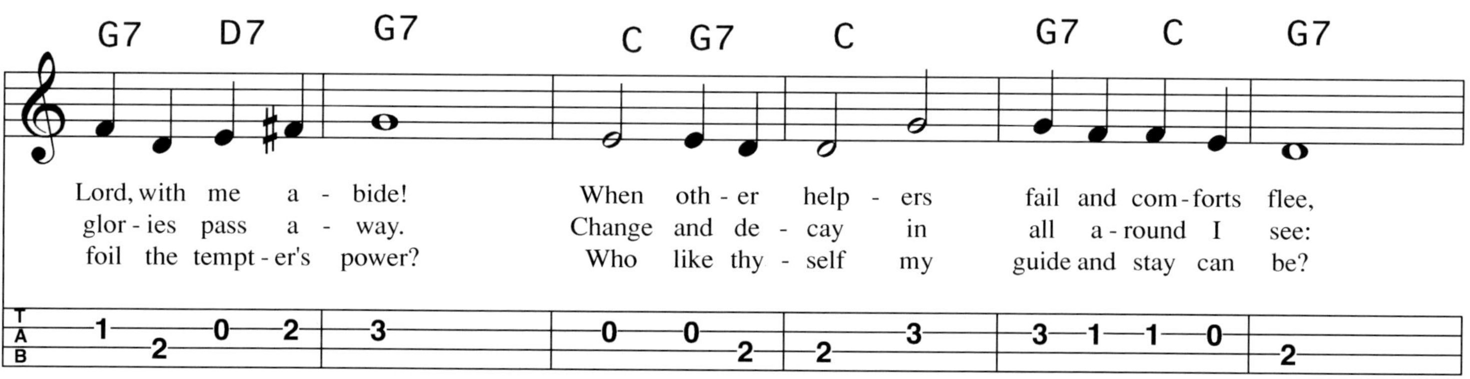

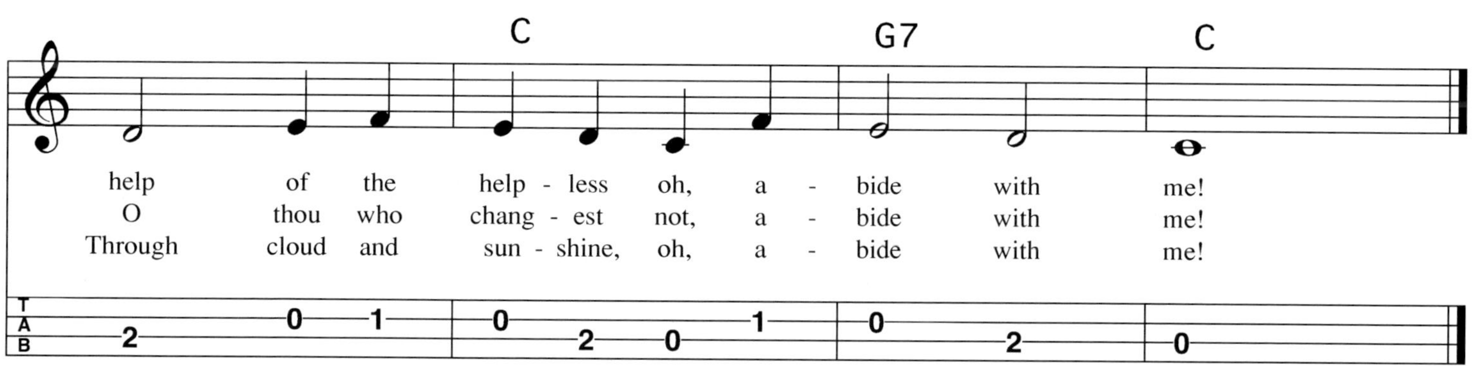

4.I fear no foe, with thee at hand to bless;
ills have no weight, and tears no bitterness.
Where is death's sting? Where, grave, thy victory?
I triumph still if thou abide with me.

When the Saints Go Marchin' In

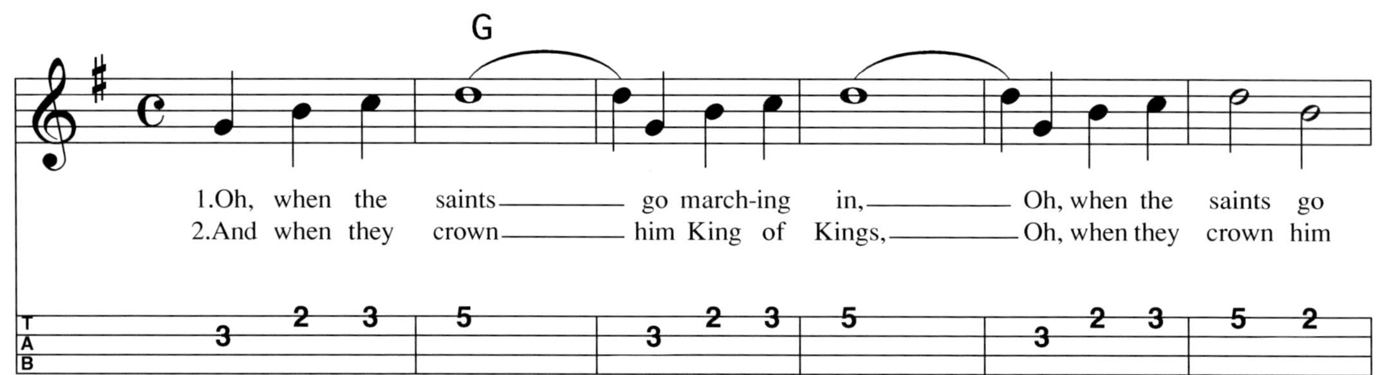

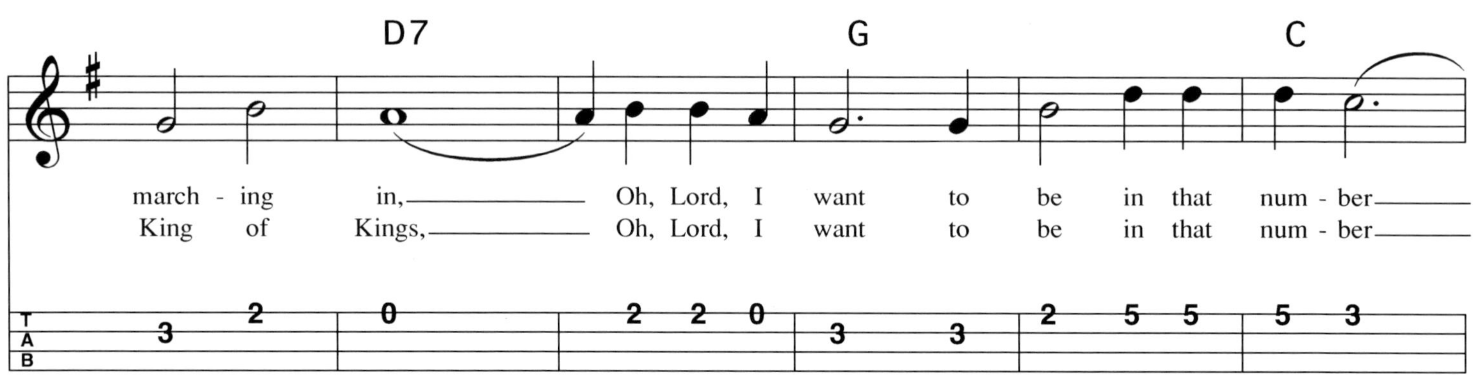

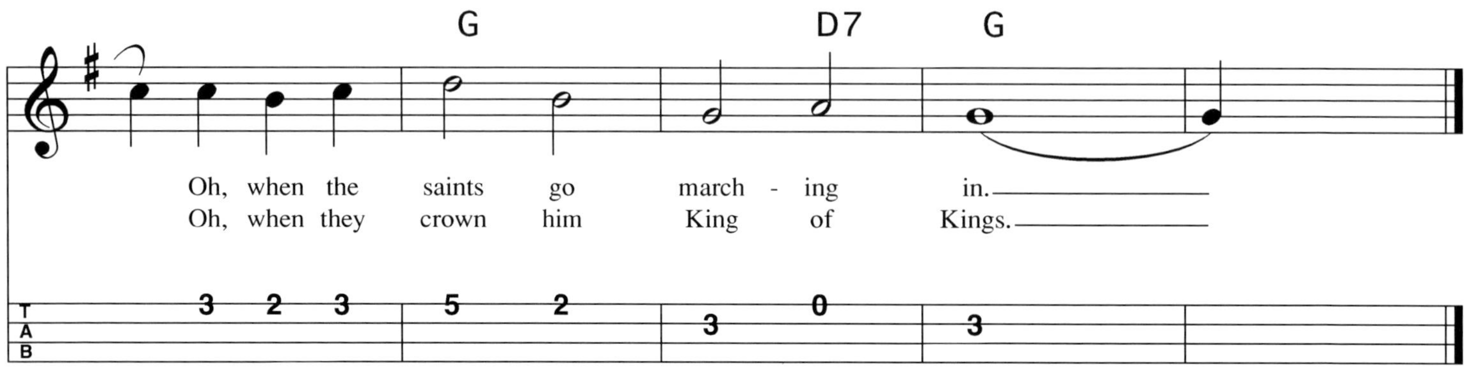

3. And when they crown Him Lord of Lords.
4. And in that Sweet By and By.

Angel of God

Ukulele Lead

Dempler

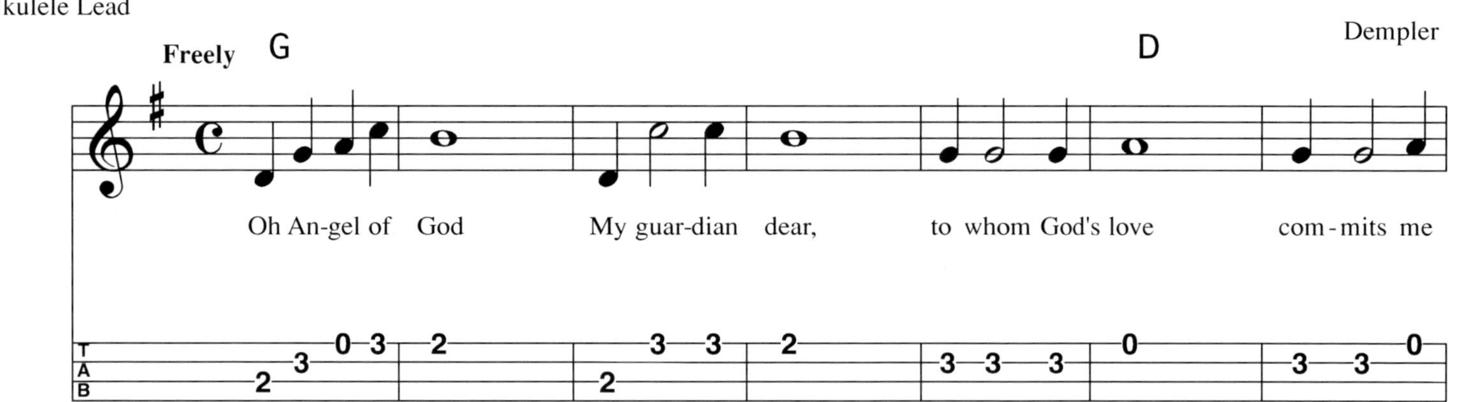

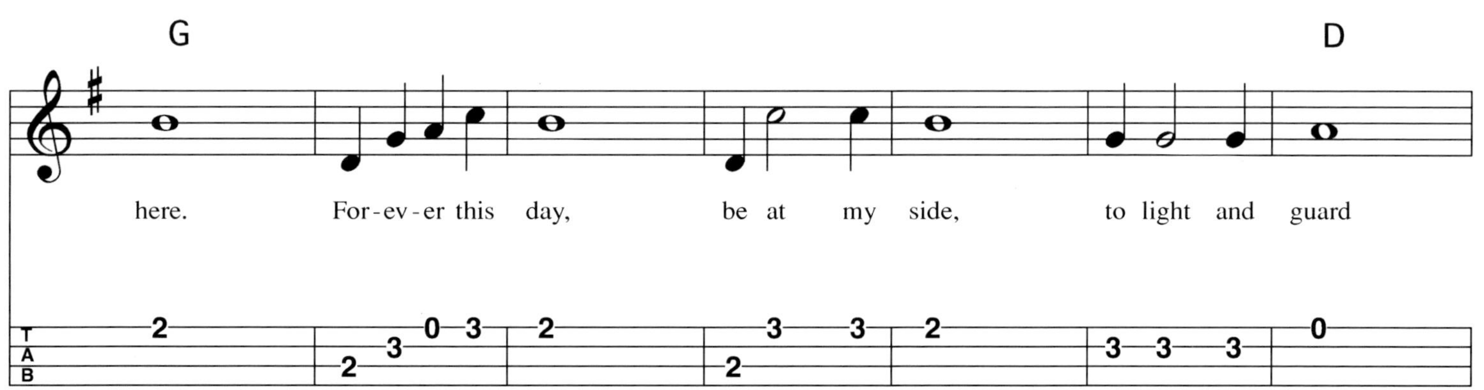

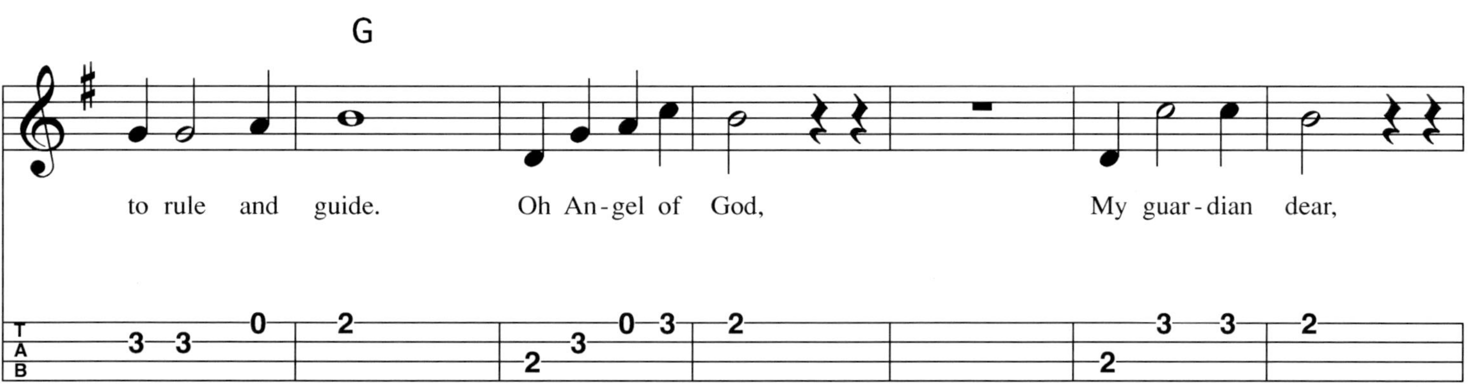

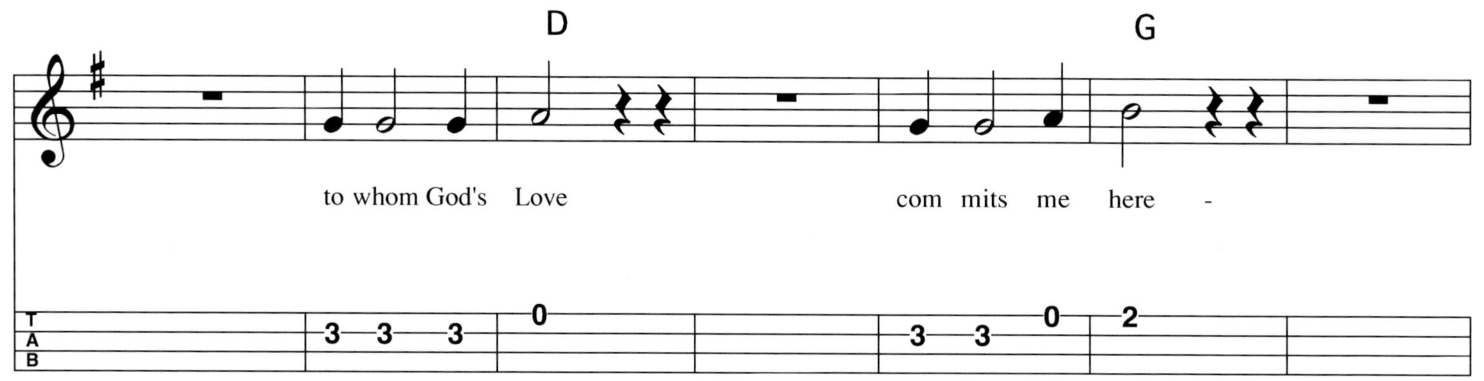
D
G
to whom God's Love
com mits me here -
T
A
B

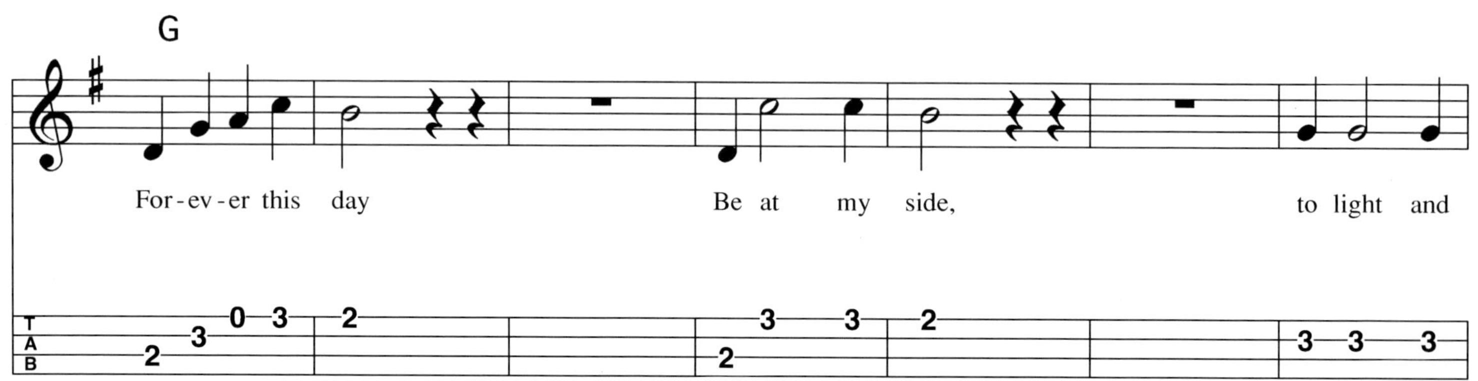
G
For-ev-er this day
Be at my side,
to light and
T
A
B

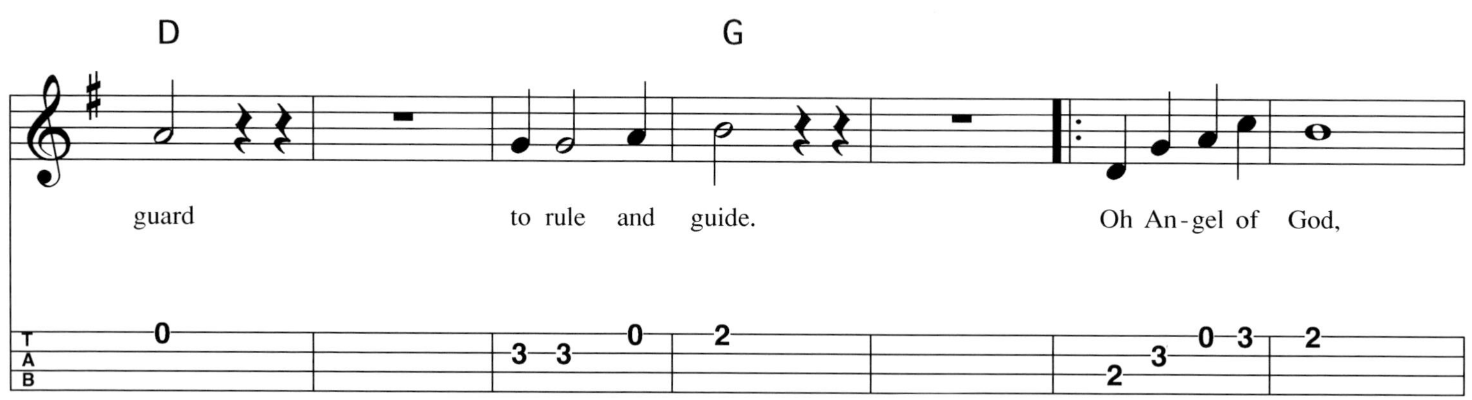
D
G
guard
to rule and guide.
Oh An-gel of God,
T
A
B

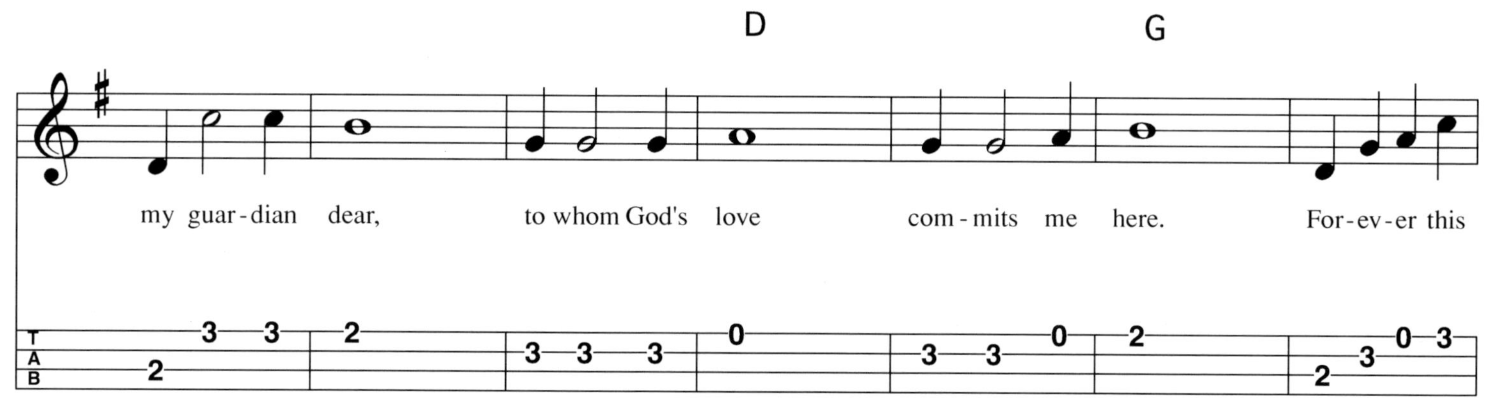
D
G
my guar-dian dear, to whom God's love com-mits me here. For-ev-er this
T
A
B
3 3 2 2 3 3 3 0 3 3 0 2 2 3 0 3

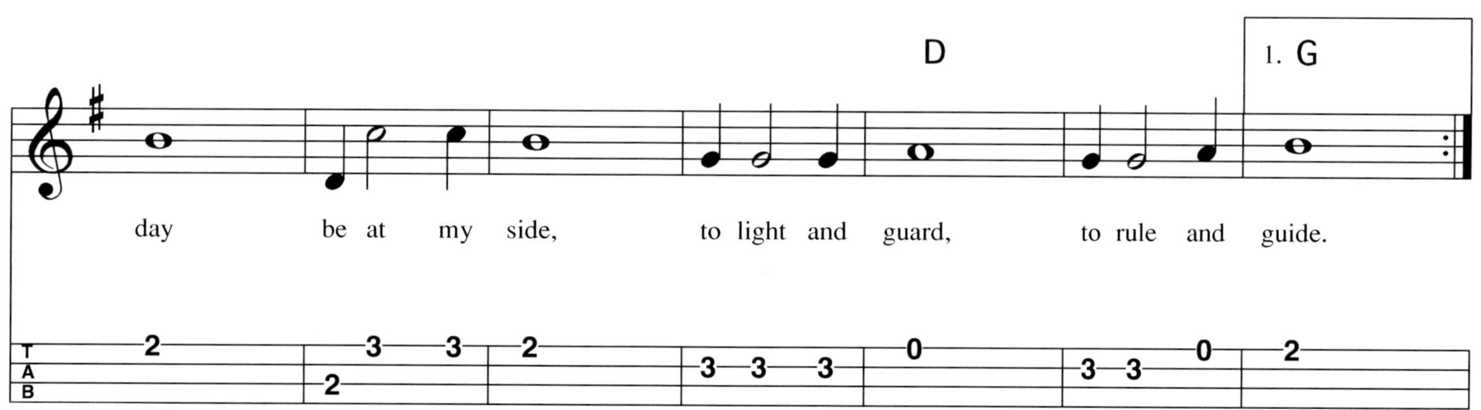
D
1. G
day be at my side, to light and guard, to rule and guide.
T
A
B
2 3 3 2 2 3 3 3 0 3 3 0 2

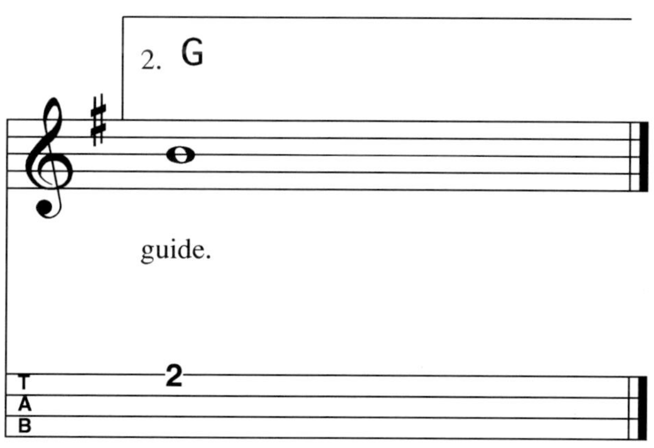
2. G
guide.
T
A
B
2

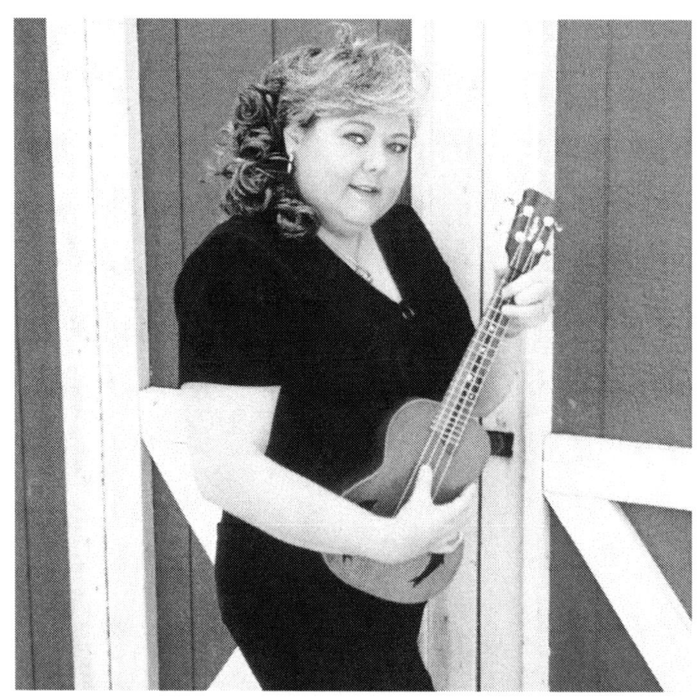

Mary Lou Stout Dempler

Kentucky's Ukulele Goddess

Mary Lou, a professional musician, studied music and guitar at Bellarmine University and obtained her Teaching Certification in Music and Dance from the Kahelelani School, recognized by the University of Hawaii. After a 22 year teaching career, she wanted to explore the ukulele world. In 1998 her husband had a ukulele custom designed and handmade for her birthday. Mary Lou fell in love with its gentle harp-like sound. In the Fall of 1998, she accepted an invitation to a ukulele workshop at Harvard University. She is a member of the Ukulele Hall of Fame Museum. Mary Lou, in an effort to promote ukulele music, recorded two albums to showcase the instruments versatility by performing rock, swing, jazz, folk, country, Christian and contemporary music. The two albums are "Songs From The Heart" and "Unique Ukulele Christmas". Both albums are in the Ukulele Hall of Fame Museum as well as the "Lou Lou" Ukulele made for and named after Mary Lou. Her next CD is "Praise the Lord". Upcoming releases are "Just Playing Ukulele" and "Christmas - Ukulele Style". Terry Meiners, of WHAS Radio in Louisville Kentucky, asked Mary Lou to be a guest on his show to discuss the ukulele, the albums and received a quick lesson on the air. Meiners branded Mary Lou the "Ukulele Goddess" and she has lived up to the name. Mel Bay Music Publications has published two books by Mary Lou; the "Easy Ukulele Method Book I" and "Easy Ukulele Method Book II". The books are designed for anyone, regardless of their musical background, to immediately enjoy playing music on the ukulele. Mary Lou teaches ukulele at Bellarmine University, at her private studios and presents workshops across the country. She is the founder and president of the Louisville Ukulele Association Unlimited (L.U.A.U.), a ukulele orchestra. Her musical efforts have been featured in the Courier Journal Newspapers, Louisville Magazine, Today's Woman, LEO Magazine, Louisville Music News and more. She has been included in a documentary film for HBO as a musician, teacher and ukulele enthusiast. In August 2003 Capital Records featured Mary Lou in an article with Keith Urban. It noted her unique use of his country music in her ukulele classes. Mary Lou truly believes "If our eyes are the windows to our souls, the ukulele is the door to our hearts".

For more information call Mary Lou at **(502) 479-8282** or e-mail her at **musiclou42@msn.com**